Caithness Archaeology –
Aspects of Prehistory

Caithness Archaeology –
Aspects of Prehistory

Andrew Heald & John Barber

Whittles Publishing

Published by
Whittles Publishing,
Dunbeath,
Caithness KW6 6EG,
Scotland, UK
www.whittlespublishing.com

© 2015 A. Heald & J. Barber
ISBN 978-184995-151-7

Typeset by Raspberry Creative Type
Printed and bound by CPI Group (UK) Ltd, Croydon, CR0 4YY

CONTENTS

PREFACE

Caithness, the most northerly county in mainland Britain, is one of the richest cultural landscapes in Europe. The relative geographical isolation of the area, combined with use of stone as the main building material since earliest times, has ensured the survival of a wide range of upstanding and well-preserved archaeological monuments. In the nineteenth century, Caithness was at the forefront of archaeological endeavours with many of her sites central to our understanding of Scottish prehistory. Since then, despite intermittent activity, the archaeology of Caithness has been marginalised and there is a perception that the county has only a handful of archaeological sites for any visitor to enjoy and interpret, and for the archaeologist to uncover. Whilst it is true that one still searches in vain for well-presented archaeological sites, traces of the past are visible everywhere in the county. Caithness is dominated by landscapes rich in archaeological remains of all periods; chambered cairns, stone settings, brochs, Pictish settlements, wags, castles, harbours and post-medieval settlement, amongst many others. These hidden treasures are at the soul of *Caithness Archaeology*.

Although the book is littered with archaeological sites it is neither a guide book nor a chronological overview of the county's archaeology. We, the writers, are not born and bred Caithnessians: we are incomers, interlopers in the archaeology of the county. But for the last decade we have been involved in a range of heritage projects in the county. This association has allowed us time to discover, observe and consider its archaeology. Our peregrinations have provided opportunities for deeper contemplation of the county's archaeology, some of which are presented in the new interpretations and perspectives we offer here. Equally, we have met people who work tirelessly for the betterment of the community and for the archaeology of Caithness. There are personalities amongst them who are worthy successors to the great Victorian antiquaries and who are at least as passionate about the county and its heritage.

Andrew Heald began work in Caithness co-directing the Caithness Brochs Project and was appointed the Caithness Archaeological Trust's first Archaeological Development Officer. He was Curator of Later Prehistory in the National Museums Scotland and is now Managing Director of AOC Archaeology Group. He dedicates this work to Kate, Danny and Lottie.

John Barber is Chairman of AOC Archaeology Group. He became involved in the county initially through the Chambered Cairn Reconstruction Project at Spittal and the Caithness Brochs Project. Since then he has engrossed himself in the county being involved in a myriad of projects and principal instigator in the ambitious River of Stone Project. John dedicates this book to Sam and Molly.

Acknowledgements
Thanks are due in particular to the Castle of Mey, Welbeck Estates and Murray Lamont of MacKays Hotel for their support of this project and to Caithness & Sutherland Enterprise for grant assistance. Appreciation is due to the following for help either financiallly or in kind: UKAEA, National Museums Scotland, nfp Synergy, npower,. Caithness Archaeological Trust and local donations at events.

1. INTRODUCTION

Caithness is the most northerly county in mainland Britain. It sits within the internationally renowned Atlantic area of Scotland, defined here as the Northern Isles, Orkney, Caithness, Sutherland, Argyll and the Inner and Outer Hebrides (Fig. 1.1). The area is one of the richest cultural landscapes in Europe. The relative geographical isolation of the county, combined with use of stone as the main building material since earliest times, has ensured the survival of a wide range of upstanding and well-preserved archaeological monuments. Although there is some evidence of regional variation, the Atlantic area features broadly similar cultural trajectories between $c.8000$ BC to $c.$AD 1100, which are manifested in the largely comparable assemblages of archaeological sites, deposits and remains.

Academic interest in the Atlantic area has focussed almost exclusively on Orkney: some of archaeology's best-known scholars – V. G. Childe and C. Renfrew, inter alios – have studied its rich remains. Other regions in the far north-east of Scotland have seen far less activity, such as Sutherland's archaeological sites, which have remained largely untouched for over a hundred years. Caithness has shared a similar fate. This has resulted in a perception that the county has only a handful of archaeological sites for any visitor to enjoy and interpret, and for the archaeologist to uncover. Whilst it is true that one still searches in vain for well-presented and properly understood archaeological sites – of the 5,000 known monuments in Caithness only a handful are under the direct care of government or local council – traces of the past are visible across the county. Caithness is dominated by landscapes that house various archaeological remains, such as chambered cairns, stone settings, brochs, Pictish settlements, wags, castles, harbours and post-medieval settlement, amongst others. It is these hidden treasures that are at the heart of this book.

The writers have been involved in numerous projects in the county. One of us (AH) began work in Caithness co-directing the Caithness Brochs Project and was then appointed the Caithness Archaeological Trust's first Archaeological Development Officer. Despite leaving the post to become the curator of Later Prehistory in the archaeology department of National Museums Scotland, AH was able to maintain enthusiasm and support for the county's archaeology with the strong support of said institution, and particularly that of David Clarke. JB became involved in the county initially through the Chambered Cairn Reconstruction Project at Spittal and the Caithness Brochs Project. Since then JB has engrossed himself in the county through

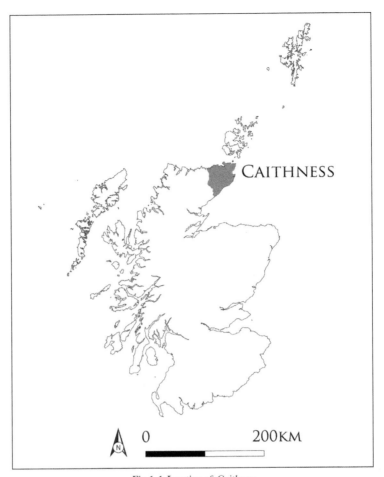

Fig 1.1 Location of Caithness

being involved in a myriad of projects and being the prime instigator of the ambitious River of Stone Project. In recent years, both authors have been involved in survey and excavation projects at Nybster, Keiss, Thrumster and Yarrows.

This association with the county has allowed us time to discover, observe and consider its archaeology. Equally, it has allowed us to experience the landscape and converse with the diverse groups of people who live across the region. For a number of years we have promised to write a book on Caithness' archaeology. One book turned into two, and then into three. We would write a guidebook with designated trails and sites to visit. We would edit an 'academic' book on the recent research programmes. Then we thought we would cut out the middleman/woman, write it ourselves and publish our work on chambered cairns and brochs. Promises, promises ...

However, there are many convenient excuses for not fulfilling promises. Yes, there is a need for an erudite synthesis that reflects and disseminates the new work that is being done in the county. There is also a crying need for a guidebook that, if nothing else, illustrates the wealth of remains in Caithness. It always infuriates us when we stay in the county's bed and breakfasts and hotels that, with very few exceptions, all literature in our rooms promotes day trips to Orkney. The archaeology of Orkney is breathtaking and well worth many visits, but surely a few leaflets on Caithness' prehistoric remains is not too much to ask for.

Apparently it is.

However, there are a number of other, more fundamental, problems in writing a leaflet or book, not least the naked truth that there are few well-kept and well-presented sites in the county. Whether we like it or not, many visitors to archaeological sites, particularly those who have travelled hundreds of miles, want settings resembling bowling lawns. They should have signposts, footpaths and parking space; the remains should be no further than 10 metres from the road and of course there must be a café. Conversely, and understandably, some individuals who own the land on which the monuments sit do not want hundreds of visitors traipsing across their ground to view some obscure bump. And let's not start on health and safety issues, and public liability. A guidebook is as problematic as they come. These are real issues, and ones that need to be addressed quickly. This book is not a guidebook and it should not be used as one. Nor is it a chronological presentation of every monument in the county. If you want a sound, academic, chronologically organised introduction to Caithness' archaeology then you can do no better than buy any of the excellent books written on the subject by the late Donald Omand: a true scholar.

Caithness Archaeology is a record of what we have learnt and experienced during our time in Caithness so far. Like any travel journal, it has many facets. Central to any chronicle are, of course the end points – the destinations – and this book is littered with archaeological sites. And when we use the word 'site', we mean it in the broadest sense – sites can be locations, arenas or landscapes. During our time in Caithness, one thing we have learnt is that the key to appreciating the county's archaeology is appreciating the landscapes in which the monuments sit. Particular settings were, and are, accorded special significance. The repeated use of specific landscapes invests areas with memory, in which past activities and people are incorporated into contemporary settings. This view has only been strengthened by AOC Archaeology's recent LiDAR surveys at Baillie and Yarrows.

But, as with many aspects of travel, often the journey to and through the various landscapes is the most enriching part of the whole experience. The pilgrimage provides many opportunities, particularly deeper contemplation of the archaeology, which, in turn, cultivates new interpretations and perspectives. The odyssey also provides the opportunity to meet a range of people: the grandfathers who spend days cutting grass on long-forgotten sites; the individuals who spend their 'retirements', often at great personal cost, working tirelessly for the good of the community; the fathers who miss family holidays to help excavate sites; the grandmothers who spend their summers making tray bakes for hungry archaeologists; and the schoolteachers who spend large parts of their holidays writing school education packs and the remainder excavating several feet down into 2,000-year-old wells – when they are not helping school children in Africa, that is. We have facts and details in this book, but if you really crave an understanding of the ins and outs of the archaeological sites and what they mean for the community you need to converse with the diverse range of individuals and groups who have lived and worked on Caithness' land for decades. By the end of this book it will be clear who some of these people are.

Equally important to the narrative is another group of people we 'meet' on our expeditions: the long gone – but not forgotten – personalities who were at the inception of the study of Caithness' archaeology. These are the people who first visited the sites; the individuals who undertook the inaugural surveys and excavations of the monuments; the characters who first lived and breathed the county's archaeology and who still survive in print, memory and folklore. This is one of the problems with academic overviews of, and guides to, a region's archaeology: they neglect the key component of any journey – that is, the people who lived and breathed the county's past and those who continue to do so. Archaeology is the study of people's past. In this book, one of our desires is to document the individuals who have studied and who continue to study and influence the archaeology of Caithness. As will become clear, many of these people were active in the mid- to late nineteenth and early twentieth centuries and we will highlight how their attitudes and methodologies shaped our understandings of the Caithness, and indeed Scottish, past. The individuals who uncovered the archaeology form as much a part of this book as the sites and landscapes we will describe, examine and interpret. In our eyes, this is critical to understanding the (pre)history of the county.

Our interest in archaeology has led us into the arms of various employers, including government institutions (Historic Scotland, National Museums Scotland), independent charities (the Caithness Archaeological Trust) and private enterprises (AOC Archaeology Group). As a result, we have encountered a number of regulations and protocols that affect the way we carry out archaeology governance and management. Whilst this is crucial to the long-term preservation of our heritage, our time in Caithness has taught us that diktat often sits uneasily with the story of the past and the hopes for the future. The average person on the street is, perhaps unsurprisingly, blissfully ignorant of regulations that we, as archaeologists, could chant in our sleep. Similarly, we have found that some bureaucracy implemented by distant authorities can cause confusion at local level. Where appropriate, we highlight some of the politics we have encountered throughout our journey.

These then, are the foundations for our book: sites, interpretations, people and politics. Many archaeologists spend months, years, decades researching the past through careful analysis of artefacts, ecofacts and structural remains. There can be no doubt that this element is critical, but their final considerations should not dominate proceedings. Rather, their findings should enhance the experience of archaeology beyond academic circles. But seldom do they. As the cook and writer Simon Hopkinson (1994, 2) says, when one prepares a meal for visitors the people are everything. There is nothing more tedious than an evening spent discussing every dish eaten in minute detail. The details – the ingredients – are, of course, the foundations, but it is the experience and, more particularly, the people, their conversations and their viewpoints, that enrich the journey. This book is a summary of what we have learnt on our journey so far.

SOME PRACTICALITIES

This book is, of course, structured around a key component: the archaeology – which is usually a site type or a particular feature encountered on a site. These form the cornerstone of the 14 main sections that form the book. Although each section has examples of the archaeology under consideration (usually around three or four monuments), the narratives are skewed and predisposed. Sometimes accounts are descriptive, dominated by overviews of the archaeological characteristics and/or the history of their recovery. At other times, conversations about the personalities who excavated the sites take precedence, and you will struggle to recall any archaeology being described. In other sections, we take the opportunity to offer new interpretations for the prehistoric remains scattered across the county. Elsewhere, other issues, such as public presentation or protection of monuments, take centre stage. Some sections are longer than others. As we have said, if you are looking for a descriptive account of every excavated chambered cairn or broch in the county, then you have bought the wrong book. In this journal we want to document the key features that we have found to be of interest about each site type, whether these relate to archaeology, people or politics. We hope the book is richer for it.

That said, we do allude to hundreds of archaeological sites throughout the book. But just because we have discussed them, it does not mean that there is anything breathtaking to see. Few monuments in Caithness are under Historic Scotland's and/or Highland Council's guardianship. Many monuments are unkempt and open to the elements. In many instances, it is difficult to decipher the original shape and construction of the monument and visitors expecting pristine sites will leave bitterly disappointed.

Which brings us to access. Just because a monument is noted in this book, it does not mean that the site can be visited freely, or that it is safe to do so. Let us be clear from the beginning, for legal reasons, that we are in no way encouraging you to visit any of the sites. But, if you do have the urge to do so, permission to have access to any land or monument should obviously be sought from the landowner or tenant upon whose ground the monument stands. In the case of a monument situated on open moorland, it is advisable to enquire about the presence and disposition of any cattle which may be in the vicinity. The Countryside Code should always be followed. It goes without saying that visitors to any monument do so at their own risk. Many of the sites are at some distance from the road and in uninhabited barren country with few passers-by. Often this can be as scary as meeting the landowner or tenant whom you forgot to ask permission from to access their land. Many sites mentioned in this book are unsafe and dangerous: it is your call.

Finally, the key point. If you do choose to visit any archaeological site, *every* monument should be treated with the utmost respect – stonework should not be disturbed, and nothing should ever be removed from any site. Very occasionally, a visitor may find something within the landscape that might be of archaeological interest: finds should be left in place and reported to The Highland Council's archaeology service. In Scotland, the law demands that any archaeological or historical find should be reported to the proper authorities, who will decide on the appropriate course of action.

Highland Archaeological Services has up-to-date information on all known monuments and may be consulted for further information on a site or landscape. In addition, the National Monuments Record at the Royal Commission on the Ancient and Historical Monuments of Scotland (RCAHMS), in Edinburgh, has detailed information for all known sites across Scotland, including Caithness.

Many of the relics found in the monuments are housed in the National Museum of Scotland, Chambers Street, Edinburgh. That said, various objects related to the monuments – particularly from the Iron Age, Early Christian and Viking periods – can be found in the county at, for example, Dunbeath Heritage Centre, Dunbeath; Caithness Horizons, Thurso; and the Caithness Broch Centre, Auckengill. Bibliographic references, where appropriate, are listed in the text.

All royalties from this edition will be donated by the authors to the Caithness Archaeological Trust to be used in future fieldwork studies.

TEN THOUSAND YEARS OF ARCHAEOLOGY IN ONE AFTERNOON

Caithness is rich in archaeological remains and within the county there are particular locations at which the concentration and diversity of remains allow the visitor to view monuments of all types and ages (see Figure 1.2). We have selected the landscape area known as Yarrows as our exemplar, and the following pages deal with the archaeology of this landscape and the history of the discovery and exploration of the area's monuments. Along the way, we try to provide you with definitions or descriptions of the monument types and, in more general terms, to introduce you to the terminology of the profession and the chronological framework within which archaeologists like to segment the past. This means that our first chapter is dense with information – albeit useful and relevant information – so please feel free to skip through it lightly, perhaps returning to it when you need some clarification on elements that crop up later in the book.

THE YARROWS LANDSCAPE

> One can scarcely go a quarter of a mile in any direction among these hills without meeting with ancient structural remains of one kind or another (Anderson 1868, 504).

Situated on the eastern coast of the county, the Yarrows and Watenan area is one of the richest concentrations of well-preserved historical and archaeological remains – of all periods – in northern mainland Britain. The absence of industrial-scale agriculture in the area has ensured the survival of important archaeological and historical monuments together with the spaces, – now fossil landscapes – in which they were built. In 1985, a survey of the area in and around Loch of Yarrows and Loch Watenan (Mercer 1985) recorded 240 sites. The recent LiDAR survey recorded many more and provides the basis for the plan shown here (Fig. 1.3).

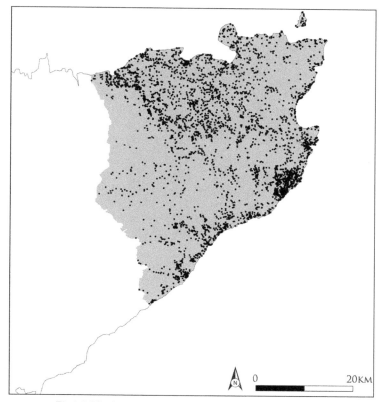

Fig 1.2 The density and richness of Caithness' archaeology

Over the last few years, evidence for Mesolithic activity has been uncovered on the Thrumster Estate by Islay MacLeod. Islay is a central figure in Caithness' archaeology. Aside from her particular interest in the Yarrows landscape, she is very passionate about the county's heritage. She was one of the central figures in starting the Caithness Archaeological Trust (CAT) and the Yarrows Heritage Trust. Islay's hospitality is legendary and we have spent many a day wandering around her home and gardens, enjoying some of the best local food. We urge you to visit her at Thrumster. It is entirely fitting that she lives in and around Yarrows. As we shall see, this is not only one of the key landscapes in Caithness archaeology but for hundreds of years has been home to, and a magnet for, people who are passionate about the area's heritage. Islay both continues and develops this long tradition.

Islay's discovery of Mesolithic flint was subsequently confirmed by Meli Pannett (Pannett & Baines 2006). The Mesolithic, or Middle Stone Age, lasted from about 8000 to 4000 BC in Scotland and was characterised by hunters/gatherers who would catch fish, hunt sea and land mammals, and collect plant food and shellfish. They fashioned tiny chipped flints, which were used singly or set in rows to form arrowheads and knives. Excavated evidence for them has been found at Oliclett. Mesolithic people appear to have built relatively slight structures in skin and wood, eg materials which of

13

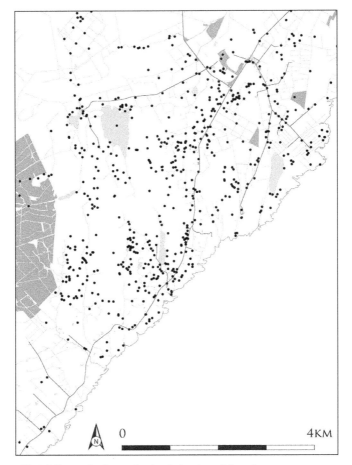

Fig 1.3 Yarrows landscape, showing the locations of the various monuments

course decay and therefore do not leave any monumental evidence (i.e. remains that are visible to the unaided eye at ground level): as a result, we speak of Mesolithic 'sites', not Mesolithic 'monuments'. The absence of monumental remains does not diminish the importance of Mesolithic sites; after all, these people were our earliest ancestors. Mesolithic settlers in Caithness had lifestyles comparable with the first peoples of North America or Australia and probably burned off areas of woodland to provide improved grazing grounds, into which the larger land mammals would concentrate and could be hunted more efficiently.

With so little direct evidence available, the Mesolithic period provides an intellectual challenge for cultural archaeologists and much ink has been spilled on the precise nature of Mesolithic people's social arrangements. In general it is believed that their population numbers were small, that they lived in small communities – possibly made up of extended families – and that the communities occupied relatively large territories around which they moved seasonally, to exploit the diffuse food resources of Scotland. There is a similarly extensive, and at times intemperate, literature on the transition from Mesolithic to the succeeding period, the Neolithic. Views range from the extermination and replacement of Mesolithic populations by Neolithic farmers to their peaceful assimilation into the new regime. For some archaeologists there was a more or less instant transition from Meso to Neo, whilst for other archaeologists the transition occurred over a protracted period with complex interactions between both periods and their peoples. These discussions, or arguments, also depend on the vehicle for the introduction of the Neolithic: was it a wave of new settlers or did the knowledge of farming arrive with only a few new people – or did it evolve spontaneously? There is no determinative evidence, so please feel free to select your very own Meso/Neo transition scenario.

The Neolithic period is characterised by the introduction of farming at, or soon after, 4000 BC. Neolithic people lived in Caithness in lightly wooded landscapes with far less bogland than currently exists and in a climate that was warmer by about two degrees centigrade. Theirs was a mixed economy, with arable and pasture in their domesticated landscapes and a reliance on hunting and gathering in the wildscapes beyond their settlements. Archaeological remains indicate that they kept cattle and pigs, and grew barley and wheat. They built complex stone monuments: the chambered cairns (Fig. 1.4). Some of these may have been intended to contain human remains, whilst others could have been built as temples – but all reverted to burial sites once abandoned, like many medieval Christian churches.

Fig 1.4 Camster Round with Camster Long in the background

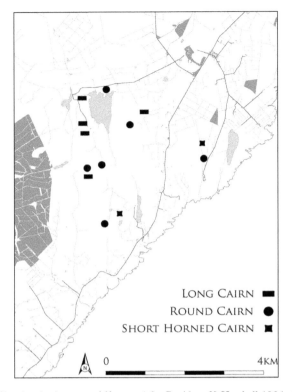

Fig 1.5 Chambered cairns around Yarrows (after Davidson & Henshall 1991, figure 6:2)

The Yarrows area is especially rich in chambered cairns as it has 18% of the county's total and one of the densest distributions: 13 cairns within an area measuring 11 square kilometres (Davidson & Henshall 1991, 14–20, Fig. 6.2, reproduced here as Fig 1.5). It is possible that some of the nearby hilltop enclosures at Garrywhin and Yarrows may have been first used at this time. This cairn-rich area was very attractive for early antiquarians, particularly Rhind, Anderson and Shearer, individuals to whom we will return to later.

At some time around 2500 BC, the transition to the Bronze Age began. This was a very gradual process and had considerable overlap with the settlements and other monuments and technologies of the Neolithic. New types of pottery vessel emerged, known as 'Beaker' pottery, and bronze tools and weapons were produced in some numbers. Objects made from gold and bronze came to represent a new form of wealth (Fig. 1.6).

In contrast with the multiple burials encountered in Neolithic chambered cairns, Bronze Age burial at first took place in individual stone-lined graves (called 'cists'). The buried body was tightly flexed, knees to chest with arms tightly folded in, and it was sometimes accompanied by pots, weapons – including arrowheads and daggers – and personal adornments, such as jet necklaces (Fig. 1.7). These were progressively replaced by cremated burials sometimes contained in large pottery urns and sometimes buried in cemeteries. These burials were often inserted into existing Neolithic chambered cairns.

Individual cist burials are usually only found by accident, often during deep ploughing. The 1987 discovery of a cist burial at Achavanich was made by a contractor digging out stone for road repairs. Following excavation and survey cists are usually removed or reburied. Thus, only a handful of these important monuments can be visually inspected by the visitor, such as the example near the stone rows at Garrywhin.

It is believed, with no good evidence, that stone settings like Garrywhin and the Hill o' Many Stanes (Fig. 1.8), were erected during the Bronze Age, together with stone circles and U-shaped settings (Fig. 1.9). The area around Yarrows and Watenan has some of Scotland's best examples of these monuments a few of which, like the stone rows, are not only unique to north-east Scotland but are also concentrated in Caithness.

Fig 1.6 The Bronze Age hoard found at Hillhead (copyright National Museums Scotland)

Fig 1.7 Cist with crouched inhumation and accompanying grave deposits, Acharole (copyright RCAHMS)

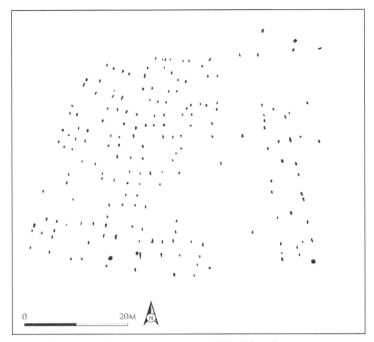

Fig 1.8 The stone alignments at the Hill o' Many Stanes

Fig 1.9 The U-shaped stone setting at Achavanich

Throughout Scotland we have direct evidence for domestic settlement amongst the Bronze Age burial and religious monuments. This takes the form of the remains of round houses with low timber or stone walls surmounted by thatched roofs. The remains are often presented as penannular (circular with gap) banks of earth – or a combination of earth and stone – and are called 'hut circles'. In the Strath of Kildonan, there are roughly 1000 hut circles and high concentrations like this are not uncommon throughout the Highlands. However, there are no matching concentrations in Caithness and indeed hut circles are rare or absent from many areas in the county. The explanation of this gap in the record demonstrates a fundamental principle in archaeological studies. The distributions of the monuments we can now observe were principally created by accidents of survival and may not be indicative of their original dispersals or numbers. We say that monument distributions are artefacts of destruction, not of creation.

In the specific case of Caithness and hut circles, we note two points: the first is that in the Highlands in general, even where there are high concentrations of hut circles, they survive above the levels of modern agricultural activity. For Caithness, this militates against their survival in the east and north of the county, which have been intensively farmed for over two centuries. The second point is that we have examples of hut circles and associated field systems and cairn fields that have 'disappeared' into deep peat deposits – and we know from work elsewhere, that peat growth accelerated at the time of the abandonment of upland hut circles. Thus, it is possible for these remains to be covered in peat and lost to view. There are extensive and deep peat deposits in

Fig 1.10 The icon of Iron Age Scotland; Mousa broch, Shetland (copyright Fraser Hunter)

the west and the south of the county. This does not leave many niches for the survival of hut circles, or indeed for other monuments, and the visitor will notice the nature of the land in the four monument-rich areas and its contribution to their endurance. That said, recent LiDAR surveys of the county revealed many new examples of hut circles that are nigh on impossible to see from ground level.

The absence of direct evidence of domestic settlement for the earlier periods is not restricted to Caithness. In general, it is believed that, like those of the Mesolithic, the Neolithic houses were built from wood or from wood and turves which, when they decay, leave no surface evidence. We need not doubt that such houses existed because the chambered-cairn builders must have lived somewhere, but it is still ironic that we know more about the dead than we do about the living in early Caithness.

Conversely, the succeeding periods are abundant in settlement evidence. Around the middle of the first millennium BC (i.e. around 500 BC) and for a further 1,000 years, impressive, thick-walled stone-built roundhouses were constructed. They differ radically from hut circles in their massive proportions– which feature walls up to 5 metres thick – and complex engineering and architecture. They were clearly designed to impress and overawe, and they represent a uniquely Scottish monumental tradition. These roundhouses include the brochs (or stone towers) like the iconic example at Mousa in Shetland (Fig. 1.10). Although these roundhouses are generally called 'brochs' it is improbable that they were all tall towers and the group includes some which could never have been significantly higher than the surviving remains. Thus, a range of

Fig 1.11 Pottery and glass recovered during excavations at Keiss (copyright National Museums Scotland)

different types lies hidden within this category of monument, ranging from full-height broch towers to more simple roundhouses. Furthermore, roundhouses were probably not the only structures built during the period 500 BC to AD 500, or thereabouts: some hilltop enclosures, promontory forts and hut circles probably date to this period also. Examples of these can be seen within the Yarrows and Watenan area.

These new structures may have been associated with changes in social structure and the emergence of warrior-aristocracy societies. This period witnessed contact between the native inhabitants and the Romans. The Romans invaded Scotland three times during the first and fourth centuries AD. Although they built forts and temporary camps in southern and central Scotland there is no evidence of this in northern Scotland, including Caithness. We know that Romans circumnavigated northern Scotland and a handful of Roman finds – mainly pottery and glass – have been recovered from the area. Roman material has been found at Keiss and other sites in the Sinclair Bay area (Fig. 1.11). It is impossible to know whether this was acquired by trade or because Romans stopped off prior to attempting to cross the treacherous Pentland Firth.

The people who populated Caithness after the Romans, between fourth and eighth centuries AD, are often labelled the 'Picts', meaning the 'painted people' – a term by which the Romans knew them. The Picts are made visible in the archaeological record by the survival of rather wonderful and very enigmatic carved stones. Earlier

Fig 1.12 The Pictish symbol stone from Ackergill (copyright National Museums Scotland)

Fig 1.13 The Pictish symbol stone with Christian iconography from Latheron (copyright National Museums Scotland)

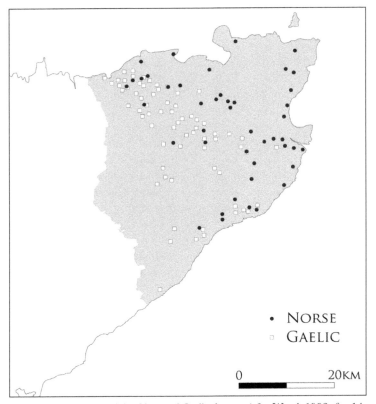

Fig 1.14 Place-names containing Norse and Gaelic elements (after Waugh 1992, figs 14 and 15).

examples of the Pictish carved stones (Class I) are unworked slabs or boulders with symbols cut into one face (Fig. 1.12). Some of the symbols are recognisable, such as fish; others are harder to interpret. Later examples (Class II) bear the Christian cross (Fig. 1.13). Other evidence for Pictish activity is not understood so well, although various graves; artefacts and buildings may relate to this period. Again, the Yarrows area has examples of all of these.

This is not the place to enter into a rigorous debate on the Picts, but you may be interested to know that the archaeological 'Pictish culture' is a fine example of reification. This is the physiological process of logical infelicity that leads us to equate the symbol for something with the thing itself. The evidence that identifies these people as 'Picts' lies in a classical reference from AD 297 and a second, but uncertain, reference from AD 310. From this slender base a whole people have been manufactured. 'Picti' was probably a soldier's slang term for everyone north of the Forth and it subsumed a range of different peoples under a single name. Even by the fifth century, on Adamnan's account, we have evidence for several individual tribes in the area, including the Scoti (the Irish), in what is now called Scotland. There is probably no great harm in the innocently misleading archaeo/historic creation of the 'Pictish people' apart from the tendency to emphasise their differences from the rest of the contemporary populations of these islands, when in fact these divergences are often trivial and are usually more apparent than real. The tendency of New Agers and their ilk to fasten onto the ideal of 'Pictishness' in establishing an identity for Scotland that excludes the traditional 'hairy-kneed Highlander' is a bit more insidious. Maud Gonne MacBride and her salon of poets and painters created a comparable Celtic myth for Ireland that was used to give the Irish a way of identifying themselves as independent of their British colonisers. In the longer term, this pollution of the clear streams of history was washed away by further study and analysis and no doubt, in time, the Picts – popular and academic – will resume more realistic proportions.

Towards the end of the eighth century, Viking raids began on the Scottish islands and mainland coasts; sometime later settlements of Norse people (i.e. people of Scandinavian origin and their immediate successors), became established throughout the area. The earls of Orkney held Orkney from the king of Norway and the area now called Caithness and Sutherland from the king of Scotland. Although it is likely that there were many Norse farmsteads in the area, only a handful have been identified in northern mainland Scotland. Similarly, Viking and Norse graves are rare in the area, albeit that some good examples have been recorded. This paucity of physical remains is offset by the abundance of place-name evidence, which shows something of the extent of the areas once inhabited by Pictish, Norse and Gaelic-speaking peoples. The place names indicate a concentration of Scandinavian influence in the northeast of the modern county, with the more indigenous population restricted to inland areas. The parish of Canisbay has a particular wealth of Norse place names, with virtually all names being of Norse origin, which implies a level of Norse settlement sufficient to extinguish all pre-Norse place names (Fig. 1.14).

During the 12th and 13th centuries the kings of Scotland made determined, and ultimately successful, efforts to extend their authority to the northern mainland. By the time of Alexander III (1249–86) Caithness, although still linked with the Norse earldom of Orkney, was considered an integral part of the Scottish kingdom.

In the period between the end of Norse dominance and the Jacobite risings, the settlement of Caithness becomes relatively invisible to the archaeologist. Faced with similar difficulties in the Outer Hebrides, Iain Crawford undertook a major study of the settlements in that area and concluded that the medieval settlements were in fact present, but masked by the later settlements of the pre-clearance period. The medieval and post-medieval periods were extraordinarily difficult times for the rural population of northern Scotland. With the incipient availability of written documents it would be easy to mistake the period for one of jolly japes in nice castles and fortified homesteads. However, for the majority of the population, especially during the little ice age, conditions were very poor and physical hardship was the norm.

Before the Jacobite risings in the early eighteenth century, the rural economy of the north of Scotland was not much more advanced than it had been in the medieval period. Chieftains and landowners tended to measure their wealth by counting their followers and dependants, and cattle on the hoof. Increasing population pressure cut into the margins and reduced the cash-equivalent value of the land, which in turn reduced the disposable income of the landowners. The Jacobite risings of 1715, 1719

Fig 1.15 The steps at Whaligoe

and 1745 led to a determined effort by the government to integrate the Highlands with the rest of Scotland. The hereditary jurisdictions of local chiefs were abolished and communications were opened up, first via military routes and then by parliamentary means.

The 18th century saw continuing population growth with, in many areas, increased demand on resources for local consumption. In some areas farming could not cope with demand, and economic emigration occurred. Some landlords became bankrupt whilst trying to support and feed their tenants and some even took in tenants cleared from other areas. However, many landlords simply evicted their tenants from the farms, especially the poorer farms on their estates, to create new and more profitable sheep farms. Clearances continued spasmodically until halted by the Crofters' Holdings Act of 1886, but this did not alleviate the conditions that led to depopulation of many rural areas. The clearances and the advent of large-scale sheep farming improved the cash flow in the rural economy; from the eighteenth century onwards, large houses were built by the landowners, new stone bridges were erected and access to lands was improved, as demonstrated by the now abandoned railways and dams, examples of which can be seen at Watenan.

During the eighteenth and nineteenth centuries hitherto small-scale rural industries were, with the availability of capital in the landed classes, moved over to a more industrial and commercial basis. In Caithness, stone for paving was quarried on a commercial scale for the first time and wherever there were outcrops of limestone, limekilns were set up. The evidence for quarrying is ubiquitous in the Caithness landscape. Landowners progressively extended their commercial activities into the exploitation of natural resources, and piers and harbours were built, or rebuilt and extended, for the growing fishing industry. One fine example exists at Whailgoe, near Watenan: a fishing harbour formed within an improbable – and downright dangerous – narrow rocky defile that must have been unapproachable in onshore winds or high seas. Even for vessels in port, it was equally hazardous and the visitor will note the iron rings set high in the cliff face to facilitate the lifting of the boats right out of the water. A flight of some 330 flagstone steps descends the precipitous cliffs from the fish-curing station above, to the quay below (Fig. 1.15). The cliffs on the east coast of Caithness are dramatically photogenic but very unfriendly to sea-going vessels, and all but the smallest boats have to find their harbours elsewhere.

Where grain was grown, the milling process similarly moved up in scale and larger watermills were constructed, some of them with corn-drying kilns attached, as at Whailgoe.

MONUMENTS IN THE LANDSCAPE

The existential navel-gazing of archaeologists is, rightly, risible, and nowhere more prolific than in consideration of the landscape setting of monuments. Some argue, for example, that landscapes are reservoirs of cultural memory, built upon by succeeding generations, each constrained and inspired by what went before. For others, the landscape is the monument and the built elements mere footnotes. The true significance of the landscape and its monuments can only be comprehended, these arguments suggest, in terms of the social values of their builders. However, the protagonists of this line go on to suggest that the social values of the builders may be inferred from the landscape contexts of their structures: circularity, or what?

Determinism is the belief that one factor completely explains a situation and determinism is not new to archaeology. In the past we explained each new wave of monuments as indicative of new waves of people moving into the area and making the changes we observe (the Invasion Hypothesis). More recently, we explained the location and sequencing of monuments in terms of climatic and other environmental factors (Environmental Determinism). We have also explained the abandonment of upland settlements in terms of climate alone (Climatic Determinism). Now we seem to be obliged to offer explanation and interpretation in terms only of social forms and norms and this is, of course, Social Determinism. Like its predecessor fads, it contains a kernel of veracity and it is a useful explanatory model in some instances. And, like its predecessors, its widespread application creates nonsense and, happily, sows the seeds of its own demolition.

Perhaps a time will arrive when we, as a profession, can accept that humanity is complex and subject to intricate motivations in all of its activities. Humanity's choices are not usually random and they are rarely whimsical but because they pursue cognate ends, the outcomes regularly create patterns – of form, distribution, etc. – over time. We suggest that, as a visitor, you observe these in whatever terms suit you best: deterministic or not. However, and more importantly, we hope that you can view the activities of our common ancestors with compassion, and with the understanding of equals. The past may be a foreign country but it is only that: it is not an alien space. The colonial condescension that characterised our approach to first peoples throughout the world is as unwelcome in consideration of humanity's past as it is offensive in consideration of humanity's present. It is, we submit, unrealistic to apply to past communities concepts of social agency or environmental, social or political powerlessness that we would not apply to living western European communities. Conversely, in accepting that our ancestors were closely akin to ourselves, we positively invite you to immerse yourself in the heritage of this area. Try to experience it as fully in emotional and aesthetic terms as you can intellectually and then to arrive at your understanding of the relationship between people and place that has occurred in this area over time.

2. A RELIGION, A CALLING, AN OBSESSION

> Caithness holds a prominent place in Archaeological Science among the counties of Scotland. For antiquarian research many sons of the county have shown aptitude and genius. In the cultivation of old world tastes there has never been any lack of enthusiasm and perseverance (Mowat 1912, 9).

Aside from being an exemplary area to visit, the Yarrows area is memorable to one of us (AH) for another reason: it was where I conducted my negotiations for the Caithness Archaeological Trust's (CAT) Archaeological Development Officer post, the interview for which was sprung on me during the 2002 Council for Scottish Archaeology's (CSA, now Archaeology Scotland) summer excursion. I remember perching behind a minibus with Lord Malcolm Caithness, who was then chairman of CAT, whilst the CSA explorers were visiting the nearby broch and cairns. Spurred on by the previous night's alcohol, and words of wisdom from a certain Irishman, I negotiated and agreed the job. I probably should have discussed it with my wife.

One of the main reasons I took the job was because I was interested in the challenge: the need to adjust the perception of Caithness' archaeology to match the physical reality. Given that my job would be to promote the county, it was a good sign that the CSA cohort was in town. If nothing else they would surely return to the central belt and tell some people about the archaeology they had seen. As the weekend progressed, it became clear that the main reason why they would talk effusively about the area, aside from the archaeology, was because of the local people – the personalities who organised and made the whole archaeological experience so memorable. The same perception was true for the members of other groups who visited in the following years: for example, the Neolithic Studies Group, the Prehistoric Society, the Northern Studies Group, the Pictish Arts Society, and the returning CSA members. The locals were as central to the whole experience as the archaeology; they knew how good their archaeology was.

The trouble was nobody else did.

Few practioners outwith Caithness hold the county's archaeology in such high regard. This perception is due not to the poor quality of the archaeological remains but because few individuals have studied the region in detail. Some haven't even visited, save to catch the ferry to Orkney. Over the last century, academics have focussed on other areas of northern Scotland. The tourists have followed suit. But those few individuals and groups who have studied the area in recent times have demonstrated how rich the county is with archaeology. The programmes of survey, by the universities of Edinburgh, Durham and Glasgow (Mercer 1980; 1981; 1985; Batey 1984; Morrison 1996) have mapped the record. As we have noted, evidence for the earliest human occupation of northern mainland Scotland has been uncovered around Yarrows (Pannett & Baines 2006) and 2002 heralded the first modern excavations of a Bronze Age stone row at Battle Moss (Baines, Brophy & Pannett 2003). The seminal study of Caithness Iron Age roundhouses by MacKie (2000; 2007) will provide the foundation for any interpretations for years to come and will be complimented by additional research programmes (e.g. Heald & Jackson 2001; Heald & Jackson 2002; Baines 2002; Barber, Cavers & Heald forthcoming; Cavers, Heald & Barber forthcoming). The Pictish period is also better understood, particularly 'wags', Caithness' own leitmotif site type (Baines 1999), whilst scholars of the Early Christian period have been encouraged by recent work at Ballachly by Lloyd Laing (2013). Work at Freswick (Batey 1987b; Morris, Batey & Rackham 1995), Dunnet (Pollard 1999) and Robertshaven (Barrett 1992; 1997) has breathed new life into the Late Iron Age and Viking periods.

All this academic research is terribly important. But arguably one of the most significant developments of the last few years has been the establishment of the Caithness Archaeological Trust, which was set up in 2002 to promote and coordinate the development of all aspects of archaeology in Caithness. CAT aims to re-engage the people of Caithness with their heritage and cultural roots in a positive way – not only as spectators, but as active participants in the development and conservation of an increasingly threatened cultural resource. Overall, the Trust wishes to develop the Caithness archaeological heritage as a cultural and economic resource for the benefit of the local community. It also hopes to promote the archaeology of the area to bodies outwith Caithness and aims to engage with all communities, interested groups, trusts, educational establishments, businesses, individuals and other bodies with similar or parallel interests. Since its inauguration, the Trust has set up a number of initiatives in which the involvement of local people and communities in the recording, preservation and conservation of sites is essential. These include: fieldwalking and excavation; an education service on local archaeology for local primary and secondary schools; the operation of branches of the Young Archaeologists Club; the organisation of lectures, conferences and summer schools; and the creation of the Caithness Broch Centre.

The considerable advances that have been made in the appreciation of the county's archaeology are thanks to CAT and its affiliates. The people involved have a 'hands-on' approach to their archaeology and are strong advocates for their heritage. They are the people who other Caithnessians turn to for archaeological advice. And they put their money where their mouths are – they often find the sites and objects that create the archaeological story. Their interest is like a religion, a calling, an obsession.

BALLACHLY

One of the major socio-political events to transform Scotland in the post-Roman period was the spread and adoption of Christianity. In a northern mainland context no narrative is complete without reference to St Columba, the priest upheld as converting the northern Picts. The various sculptured stones carved and erected by the Picts, particularly those with crosses on them, represent some of the best evidence for the adoption of the new ideology. These are carved in relief, usually on carefully shaped and dressed stones. The use of the cross and symbols are associated with the conversion of the local population to Christianity. Fine Caithness examples are the stones from Ulbster, Skinnet and Latheron (see Blackie & Macaulay 1998 for a useful summary).

Other sculptured crosses, which lack Pictish symbols, have also been found across the county. A fine example was found built into the wall of a mausoleum in the graveyard at Old Reay. Although they may be contemporary with the Pictish stones, some examples may be associated with the presence of Irish priests, who had travelled to the county during the spread of Christianity. The incised boulder at Lybster, and the crosses at Clach na Ciplich, Skinnet and Mid-Clyth may fall into this group. Few visible traces of the priests' monastic buildings remain, although there are tantalising possibilities.

One key area in any story of Caithness' archaeology – and for now, we are concerned with evidence for religion – is Ballachly, Dunbeath. Here a possible chapel sits on a natural mound, which is associated with a massive enclosure wall. Bishop Forbes noted in 1762 that here 'had been a small monastery of old called the Chapel or Church of Peace'. Credence is lent to this suggestion by the recovery of a sculptured stone fragment, in a nearby outbuilding, in 1996. The carving consists of three arms of a cross and part of the fourth arm, plus a fish between two of the arms. Crosses of this style are comparatively rare in Scotland.

Aside from the importance of the stone, the site also links us with a key family: the Bethunes. The stone was discovered when George, husband of Nan, was demolishing an old outbuilding on their land, just uphill from the chapel site. It is fitting that it should be they who discovered the carving. Nan and George have always been deeply involved in Caithness' archaeology, were central to the creation of the Caithness Archaeological Trust and regularly organised Scottish Archaeology Month and Highland Archaeology Week events for many years.

ST JOHN'S POINT

Local experts are not new to Caithness. Nan and George follow a long tradition of locals who are and who were passionate about their heritage, who studied the remains, who excavated them and, more importantly, disseminated the information both within and beyond the county's boundaries. It is because of these individuals that people living in the county today can argue the importance of their heritage. Because of them, the archaeological potential of Caithness has never been in doubt.

One of the unsung heroes of Caithness archaeology in the late nineteenth and early twentieth centuries was John Nicolson. A farmer by profession, Nicolson was also a renowned sculptor and artist who spent much of his life at the Half Way House in Auckengill, a small village between John O'Groats and Wick.

Nicolson had a keen interest in prehistory and history. During the fishing season, Nicolson used a horse and cart to collect salmon from the small harbours between Mey and Keiss and deliver them to Wick. It was on these journeys that he made observations of possible archaeological sites across the north and east coasts. These surveys stirred his interest in the county's remains, particularly in and around his home area.

In 1919 Nicolson excavated a chapel situated in the promontory fort at St John's Point, about a mile east of the Castle of Mey. He uncovered the inner face of the building, laying bare the western gable. Digging near the doorway he came across a slab-lined grave, of which one side was part of a cross-slab (Fig. 2.1). The slab was decorated with a plain, incised cross and the whole design was enclosed within a rectangular panel (Blackie & Macaulay 1998, 16). It is difficult to date the stone with any certainty. Drawing on his artistic skills he sketched the find and then it was moved to Barrogill Castle for preservation. He published the work a few years later (Nicholson 1922; Lamb 1980).

This small-scale episode sums up Nicolson's attributes. He traversed and surveyed the landscape, looking for potential sites of interest. Once a site was found he undertook excavation. Following this, he recorded and preserved the finds and noted the structural characteristics of the architecture. He also recorded many of his excavations through a series of watercolours (fig 2.2). He then published his findings promptly and effectively.

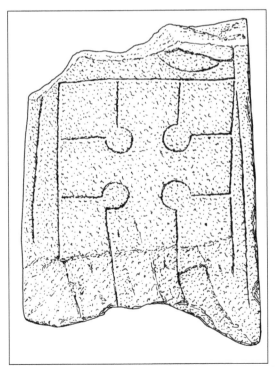

Fig 2.1 The carved stone discovered by Nicolson at St John's Point (copyright RCAHMS)

Fig 2.2 Nicolson's sketch of Kirkstones (copyright RCAHMS)

These ideals differ little from twenty-first-century archaeology.

As will become clear throughout this book, Nicolson was a pivotal figure in much of the county's archaeological work during the late nineteenth and early twentieth centuries. His contribution is usually assessed through his relationship with Sir Francis Tress Barry (see the section on brochs). Together, they excavated a number of sites, particularly brochs. Not only did he take much of the responsibility for the excavations, he is also the reason we have any idea of the structures and artefacts that were uncovered because he recorded the findings through a series of watercolours and sketches. Furthermore, Nicolson took great pride in the monuments and discoveries long after the excavation seasons were over. The commemorative monuments Nicolson and Barry constructed on the sites they excavated are some of the most endearing legacies of their work, there being no finer an example than Mervyn's Tower at Nybster (Fig. 2.3). The monument, which is 10 feet high, is decorated with sculptures, beasts and flags and adorned with Barry's name and the date of excavation, and is a solid, vernacular commemoration of their work. The primacy of the monument is shown by the fact that it was built from, and over, Iron Age structures the pair had uncovered. Barry and Nicolson felt that recording their own presence in the landscape was as important as the archaeological remains uncovered. Given that Nybster is a stone's throw from Nicolson's house it is highly probable that he maintained the site and monument in later years.

Nicolson's importance to the county should not be left in Barry's shadow, as it is often done. After Barry's death in 1907, Nicolson continued his sterling work. Although he continued to excavate brochs – he carried out excavations at Brabstermire and Hollandmey in Canisbay (RCAHMS 1911, 16, nos 37 and 39; MacKie 2007, 462, 444) – he also

Fig 2.3 Mervyn's Tower, built to commemorate Sir Francis Tress Barry's work at Nybster, Auckengill

excavated other structures from other periods. For example, he either excavated or was involved in the recording of the chambered cairn at Rattar (Davidson & Henshall 1991, 165–6) and the mysterious site of 'Poows of Kennel'. He also undertook further excavations at Moorland Mound where Samuel Laing first excavated, and referred to the site as Kirk Stones (Nicolson 1916). His watercolours and drawings were also a vehicle for recording the work of others; for example, Anstruther Davidsons's work at Coghill broch and the Acharole cist burial (see Bryce 1905 for report) were immortalised through the pen and paint of Nicolson (Fig. 1.7). His watercolours also hint at other archaeological work in the county, for example at Ackergill. Nicolson also collected antiquities and displayed or donated them to the Society of Antiquaries of Scotland; these include a bronze spearhead from Freswick and a bronze sword from Mey (discussed under the 'articles exhibited' in the *Proc Soc Antiq Scot*, 1910–11, 15–16). He was also involved in the discovery, recording and preservation of two of the most important Pictish sculptures found in northern Scotland, at Ackergill and Latheron (Blackie & Macaulay 1998, 8, 10). He even had a hand in the recording and preservation of the Bronze Age gold hoard from Hillhead (Curle 1913).

Like many of the local inhabitants of the county today, Nicolson's knowledge of the county's heritage was highly valued. There are numerous references in the literature to Nicolson being asked for advice on a range of topics (brochs, crannogs, sculpture, hoards). When surveying the county a hundred years ago, for the Royal Commission on the Ancient and Historical Monuments of Caithness Inventory, A. O. Curle consulted Nicolson about a range of archaeological issues. Nicholson was evidently an engaging personality, described in Curle's journal as:

one of the most amusing characters I have met in my wanderings … By nature he is an artist. He can draw, paint and sculpture. Though amateurish his pictures are full of humour and character, and his drawings of antiquities neat and accurate … and Caithness is much indebted to him for the exploration of its ancient structures (RCAHMS MS/36/2).

His assistance was duly acknowledged in the inventory publication (RCAHMS 1911, iv). Nicolson's importance was echoed by others: in 1935 the *Proceedings of the Society of Antiquaries of Scotland* carried an obituary for him, describing him as 'one of the best-known men in his native county of Caithness'. Such was his reputation, that he was the first to be informed of any fresh discovery in the county' (*Proc Soc Antiq Scot* 1935, 5).

Nicolson was a surveyor, an excavator, a cataloguer of finds, a preserver, a disseminator of information and a person to whom people turned for archaeological advice. We can do little but agree with Mowat (1912, 9) who, almost a hundred years ago, stated: 'when we see John Nicolson from the future, and after the lapse of years, we shall recognise the stature of his genius better than we do now'. Such sentiments may also be true for his equivalents in the twenty-first century. These are the people through which the county's archaeology is discovered, preserved and disseminated. Caithnessians living and breathing their heritage.

3. CHAMBERED CAIRNS: MANSIONS FOR THE DEAD OR TEMPLES FOR THE LIVING?

Archaeology in the twenty-first century is a slow, often tedious, process; it's a multifaceted, expensive, time-consuming discipline and both excavation and subsequent analysis involve teams of specialists, sometimes working for years. However, the most important weapons in our arsenal are the historical records of previously excavated sites through which we can compare, assess and judge the monument under exploration. Whilst it may be invidious to single out scholars for specific mention, it would be wrong not to acknowledge the work of Audrey Henshall who initially alone (Henshall 1963; 1972), and subsequently in collaboration with James Davidson (Davidson & Henshall 1991) visited, studied, catalogued, interpreted and published all of the county's Neolithic chambered cairns. Given the substantial archive of results from past excavations and surveys we now know a great deal about our past, or rather, those aspects of the past that attracted the attention of our professional (and amateur) predecessors. The early work concentrated, understandably, on the large, visible monuments to the exclusion of the small or ephemeral remains, which in every period are more numerous than the former. As noted, we have yet to discover the houses of the Neolithic population in Caithness, for example, and our knowledge of the period (roughly 4000 BC to 2000 BC) is principally derived from studies of the chambered cairns. This introduces biases into our interpretations that not only colour our view of the period, but of the monuments themselves.

The arrival of farming and the Neolithic way of life (about 4000 BC) heralded major changes for the local population. Over the following period, reliance on hunting and food gathering took second place to husbandry and cultivation, and seasonal hunting camps were replaced with settlements that were more permanent. The Neolithic is best known for the emergence of constructed monumentality and, whether intended or not, the result of this was that the monuments – the chambered cairns – changed the landscape and formed new statements or modified existing ones.

As they survive to us, chambered cairns are often impressive mounds or cairns of stone that cover varyingly complex chambers, in some of which excavation has revealed multiple burials represented by disarticulated human bones. The burials deposits rarely contain all the bones of any one individual and no patterning has been detected in the 'selection' of bones for inclusion or survival. The chamber floor deposits may also include some or all of the following: pottery, as sherds and as vessels; animal bone, usually disarticulated; bone and stone beads; bone pins; and in a few cases, carved stone basins and stone balls. Some cairns, mainly the circular variety, have a kerb of large stones at ground level around their outer perimeter and in some cases some of these kerbstones, as well as stones in the passages and chambers, may be decorated with simple patterns of circles, either single or concentric sets, and may have a central cup-mark (or dot). Spirals, linear patterns of chevrons or triangles, groups of cup marks and curvilinear lines also appear. Although individually mundane, these motifs are sometimes built into more complex forms, like the triple, interlinked spirals in Maes Howe, Orkney. There is no evidence for Megalithic art (as it is termed) in Caithness to date, but it seems likely that some will be discovered sooner or later.

A chamber was usually built by the process known as corbelling (Fig. 3.1) which means that the chamber was a hollow, formed within a 'core cairn', and this structure could stand alone as a self-supporting monument. The core cairn was then usually enclosed within a larger cairn, the 'enclosing cairn' which, in Caithness, was usually either roughly circular or trapezoidal (like a long thin triangle with its apex cut off). The shape of the core cairn was mainly determined by the shape of the chamber and these often approximate to circular or rectangular forms; additionally, circular cairns may contain rectangular core cairns, and vice versa. The chambers in Caithness were connected to the outer world via a passage which was often impossibly low, but was sometimes high enough for a person to crawl through or occasionally high enough to walk through, if the walker was stooped over. The

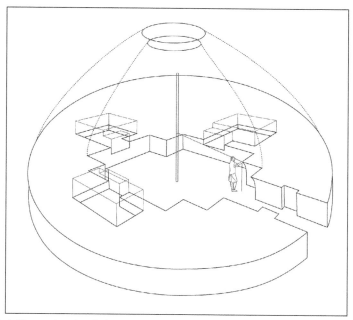

Fig 3.1 Corbelling requires that the interval voids are in balance at every level. Therefore, no scaffolding or other support is needed even in the construction of large or complex shapes

length of the passage depended mainly on the shape of the enclosing cairn, as this determined the distance between the core cairn and the outer face of the enclosing cairn.

The enclosing cairns, as they survive to us, are usually amorphous mounds of stones with poorly defined edges and variable height. However, evidence now available makes it clear that both circular and trapezoidal enclosing cairns had stepped sides; in Caithness, the excavated long cairn at Camster reveals the evidence for these wall faces around its margin. It is also visible – but to a lesser extent – at the nearby circular cairn, and the acute observer can find the line of the core cairn's external wall face within a break in the slope on the surface of the surviving amorphous mass of cairn stones. The tiered appearance of the finished enclosing cairn is usually only represented by one, two or three of the low outermost walls remaining intact around the edges of the monument, beneath the collapse of material from higher up on the original cairn – although some monuments retain rather more of this evidence. It is both interesting and possible to trace the lines of some of the 'polycope' walls in some of the Caithness cairns, and finding them enables the observer to comprehend the monuments more fully and to arrive at a more realistic appraisal of the technical abilities of their builders. These are not trivial monuments and, having built several full-scale experimental reproductions of them ourselves, we have a high regard for the human beings who originally built them.

One of us (JB) has had a lifelong fascination with ancient technologies. This came to the fore in his excavation of the chambered cairn at Point of Cott on Westray, in

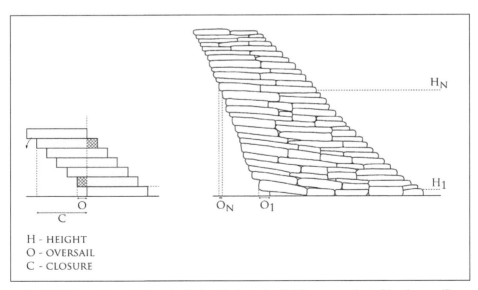

Fig 3.2 With equal oversail of regular blocks (left) the stack will fail as soon as the total length over sailing equals the length of a block. Corbelling prompts reduction in both oversail and stone thickness with increasing height (right)

the Orkney archipelago. The cairn at Cott was eroding into the sea and in danger of total loss, so Historic Scotland decided that it should be excavated in full and this presented a wonderful opportunity to study the engineering and architecture of a long cairn. Following a failed attempt to explore the understanding thus gained at Cott on a site in Orkney, the opportunity to do so in Caithness was warmly welcomed and in 2002 a community-based project was initiated in A&D Sutherland's quarry at Spittal in Caithness. The project was dedicated to experimental work on early drystone-built structures in general, and chambered cairns and brochs in particular. The point of the experimental work was simply to try to distinguish between engineering and architecture in the cairns. John Ruskin, the founding father of studies in the history of art and architecture, suggested that architecture was all the parts of a building that were not necessary for its structural stability, whilst everything else was engineering. We might quibble with this now, especially since recent developments in material science have enabled the creation and use of structural elements that can assume any shape or colour, and carry any ornamentation that we may wish to inflict on them. Nonetheless, his general thesis is that choices based on cultural preferences or fashions can only have free rein on elements that are not structurally critical. For example, however much we might wish it, we cannot build an unsupported roof; and the walls, piers, pillars, cantilevers, composite beams, tensioned fabrics, and so on, that we may use to create and support the roof cannot, in general, take unusual forms simply for artistic reasons. They can of course be ornamented in plaster, paint or any other form of decoration – but it is the embellishments, and not the structural elements, that equate to architecture in Ruskin's paradigm. Accepting Ruskin's view, we first developed a mathematical model for the limiting conditions for stability in a corbelled chamber (Fig. 3.2). Then we built several corbelled curves and measured how closely they could be made to approximate to the theoretical model (Fig. 3.3). Following that, we built a full chamber, to examine both the interplay of corbelled curves with each other and the problems associated with structural complexity (Fig. 3.4).

It is possible to build very robust corbelled structures by simply making the walls very thick (Fig. 3.5), and no doubt some Neolithic chambers were constructed in this way. However, we are now surveying existing chambers to try to establish how closely the Neolithic builder came to the limiting stability condition because we believe that closer approximation to the optimum would imply a more profound understanding on the part of the Neolithic engineer: all of which is the subject of another book.

Similarly, we have studied the degrees of freedom implicit in decision-making with regard to corbelling. For example, if we wish to build a simple beehive-shaped corbelled chamber, the determination of its radius at ground level pretty much defines everything else about it. This bears upon the issue of transferability of knowledge and helps us to explore the options that cairn building was either a specialist occupation, or one accessible to everyone. Again, the results of these and other deliberations will appear shortly in a separate book.

In contrast, once the core cairn had been built and capped off, the builders could enclose it in a cairn of any shape they wished – and it seems that they wished for circular and trapezoidal cairns. They also seem to have opted for tiered structures

Fig 3.3 The collapse in the chamber results from removal of material in the tail of the central right compartment. This patterned collapse is often mistaken as deliberate placement of sealing deposits

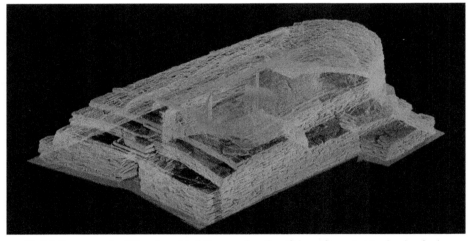

Fig 3.4 Laser scan of a full-scale model of the core cairn of an Orkney/Cromarty type chambered cairn. The core cairn which contains the chamber would then be enclosed within a trapezoidal and largely vacuous long cairn

that, in the circular cairns, look a little like elaborate wedding cakes and were much closer to a stepped pyramid than to the loose jumbles of stone that survive to us today. The long cairns had a more complex external geometry with the creation of a forecourt area between extended hornworks at the higher and wider end of the cairn. The cairns at Camster are excellent examples of both forms and if you only have time to visit one site in the county, this should be it.

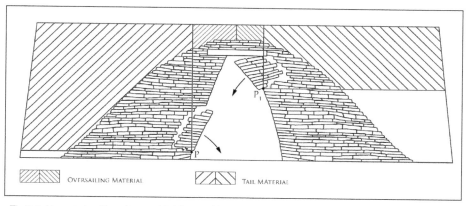

OVERSAILING MATERIAL   TAIL MATERIAL

Fig 3.5 At any point, P, on the cornel led face, stability requires that the mass of material in the tail is equal to or greater than the mass of material over sailing. Inclusion of the corbelled structure in a larger cairn or mound will preserve the stability and in fact make the structure more rigid. Conversely, the removal of modest amounts from the shoulders of the structure will rapidly destabilise it, causing collapse

In building these experimental models, we relied heavily on the vernacular skills of the local population, foremost amongst whom were Paul Humphreys, Nan and George Bethune, Meg Sinclair, Gordon Smart, Jennifer Henderson and her daughters. The building teams were given the absolute minimum of information and guidance congruent with their health and safety, in the belief that working practices and constructional challenges would emerge from the material itself: and to a large extent, this is what occurred. We could not mention Spittal without mentioning Sheila Gillen, who is incredibly passionate about Caithness and particularly her home, which is in the Spittal area. She is a remarkable, formidable woman, and one of the best we have met on this, or any, journey.

We have focussed here on the engineering and architecture of chambered cairns, but it is important also to consider the roles they played in society. The human bones found in chambers are almost exclusively disarticulated: that is, the bones are not arranged in their correct skeletal positions, but instead they lie in a great jumble on the floor intermixed with other materials and with soil accumulations. This has encouraged some archaeologists to suppose that the bodies were exposed elsewhere for the flesh to decay and that during this process of excarnation some of the bones become lost or were taken by animals, for example. Other archaeologists have suggested that bones were removed from the chambers to be used in some rite elsewhere or used as dedicatory burials in other chambered cairns. There is of course no evidence either for excarnation or for the supposed rites that required bone removal. More importantly, there is no evidence anywhere to demonstrate that the burials were the only or even the main function of the chambered cairns when they were built. It has simply been assumed that these are burial monuments. Of course we do not consider that Christian cathedrals are tombs simply because they contain burials and the interment of the 'towering dead with their nightingales and psalms' (Dylan Thomas, 'In My Craft or Sullen Art') may present a more appropriate model for thinking about burials in chambered cairns. When radiocarbon dates have been assayed for more than one or two bones from the same cairn we discover that the bones often date to periods spread over 1,000 to 2,000 years with large intervals between separate acts of bone deposition. Regrettably, the dates of the materials included in the chamber floors are the only available way to date the building of the monuments, an event with which their only relationship is that the building must have been completed at some unknown earlier time. If a large amount of radiocarbon assays are undertaken on a single tomb, we might hope or guess that the interval between the earliest burial and the date of the construction is not too long: but note that this is only a hope, unsupported by direct evidence! If only one or two dates are assayed, it is possible, but not necessarily very probable, that the earliest dated bone is from the earliest deposit of bones and therefore it is unrealistic to base our dating of chambered cairns on such shaky grounds.

Viewed as an architectural phenomenon, the close parallels – which amount to architectural and engineering coherence – between chambered cairns of all types along the whole of the Atlantic facade from North Africa to Norway, suggests that they were all built within a relatively short period. That period is likely to have been before the earliest of the dates available from chamber contents and our best guess at this time would be a date range that starts close to 4000 BC and ends within a few centuries.

We have already noted that the distribution of chambered cairns in Caithness is concentrated in four areas with a diffuse spread over the rest of the county. On the basis of evidence from Denmark and elsewhere, we may deduce that the surviving cairns are likely to amount to no more than one twentieth of the number originally built. Therefore, what survives is a distribution that results from survival, rather than creation. It has long been noted, for example, that the distribution of cairns in the islands of the Orkney archipelago is inversely proportional to the land values of the individual islands. Thus, the islands that are agriculturally richer have fewer chambered cairns, whilst those with poor quality land have higher numbers of cairns surviving. Furthermore, the cairns surviving on the best land tend to be the largest examples, implying that all the smaller ones have been removed to clear land whilst the effort involved in removing the largest cairns, like Maes Howe, would not be justified by the modest area of land released for cultivation. Perversely, the densest surviving clusters of archaeological remains are not indicative of the optimal areas for human settlement but of the areas that have always been, and continue to be, the most marginal.

One consequence of the higher survival rate for chambered cairns in marginal areas is that many of them are located in highland areas. Some Caithness cairns survive in clusters that are gathered around hills, lochs or rivers. Renfrew (1979), and others, have argued that chambered cairns may have defined territories or established entitlement to communities' claims to an area of land. Phillips (2002) has argued that the cairns are dominant markers within the wider landscape, that they are visually interconnected and that, in effect, they redefine the landscape with their presence; their situation in prominent positions allowed them to be seen from a distance and, in this way, they may have dominated the landscape and the people who lived amongst them.

Regrettably, reality is somewhat more mundane. Henshall's surveys and work done by others have demonstrated that even when sited on high ground, chambered cairns are not usually positioned on the highest points available in the locality. Typically, they lie below the nearest summit and are often on natural – or perhaps in some cases, artificial – platforms cut back into the hill slope. Even when located at significant elevations, the cairns are usually too small to be visually dominant in the wider landscape although, when complete, they may have been more easily identifiable over short distances.

Much of the work on the intervisibility of monuments, especially in Caithness (Phillips 2002), was undertaken without the use of Geographical Information System (GIS) software, which can calculate and map the zones of theoretical visibility of monuments in the landscape. Note the use of the term 'theoretical' in this phrase, because even modern mapping is too imprecise to include every minor undulation in the landscape and many objects mapped as theoretically intervisible cannot in reality be seen from each other's position. If we also include the presence of vegetation in the landscape, especially trees and hedgerows, the mapped intervisibility becomes even more theoretical. The visitor can see for themselves just how intervisible these monuments actually are, but should be prepared for disappointment. Some researchers, like Phillips, suggest that the positioning of monuments in the landscape was actually undertaken in order to demonstrate this characteristic of intervisibility. However, recent work has shown that if we randomly select groups of locations in the landscape that are in all respects similar to those occupied by monuments, we get the same – or greater – levels of theoretical intervisibility as those demonstrated in the existing monuments. Thus, there is no support in the data for the suggestion that intervisibility was a criterion in the selection of a building site for any one monument.

All that said, it is unlikely that the building sites for chambered cairns were randomly selected, although it is impossible to demonstrate this, given that the greater part of the original distribution is absent. Our experience has been that the locations of cairns are often intimate spaces, even when sited on or close to hilltops. Indeed, sites on gently rounded hilltops are often hidden from the immediately local area because of the curvature of the hill. These then present a somewhat theatrical revelation of the monument, which appears to pop out of the ground at very close range. Our friend and colleague Kim Wilson, the sculptor, has shared with us her perceptions of the factors that contribute to a sense of the sacredness of places. In reduction, these amount to factors that afford access to a sense of the infinite in our universe and our connectedness to it. In looking, for example, at the henge of Cairnpapple, near Edinburgh, the monument is sited on the top of a convex hill, invisible from its immediate neighbourhood in almost all directions. Standing within the henge, the local sub-horizon is very close in and the views beyond it are quite distant. This creates a sense of being in a saucer and floating over that distant landscape. The skies above are uninterruptedly visible in all directions and even in daylight the ambience of the place is tangible. One is protected in an intimate, close setting, but connected to the limitless universe in a spiritual and psychological way that invites further thought and study. We are aware of several other cairns from which the sense of close boundedness and infinite access sit side by side to create a strong emotional impact on the viewer. We are also acutely aware that none of this emotional understanding of the monument is testable and much of it may be *sui generis* to the individual visitor, with the same site providing some visitors with deeply moving experiences whilst leaving others unmoved. It is also possible that in some instances, and probably in the case of Cairnpapple, the presence of the monument is a factor in our modern appreciation of the landscape setting of the monument. Whether or not we can attribute to Neolithic cairn-builders the prescience required to select natural flora into which the introduction of a monument would provide the final link to the boundlessness of creation is not a question which any of us can answer with confidence, but it would be nice to think so.

WAREHOUSE SOUTH, NORTH AND EAST

When entering Caithness from the south and driving towards Wick, the visitor will eventually see a prominent ridge on the left, which stands 180 metres above sea level, in and around the area of Yarrows. Amongst the monuments along this ridge are the stone cairns known locally as Warehouse South, Warehouse North and Warehouse East (Fig. 3.6) and all three can fit within a circle of 200-metre radius. The three Warehouse cairns were first excavated by Alexander H. Rhind (Fig. 3.7). Born in 1833, he was the son of Josiah Rhind, a well-known banker and the proprietor of Sibster farm, near Wick, which afterwards became the possession of his son (Mowat 1912, 9). Rhind undertook some of the earliest and most important archaeological work in the county. After studying at Pultneytown Academy, Rhind went to Edinburgh University at the age of fifteen to study natural history and philosophy. During this time, and during extensive travels in Britain and abroad, he acquired a wide knowledge

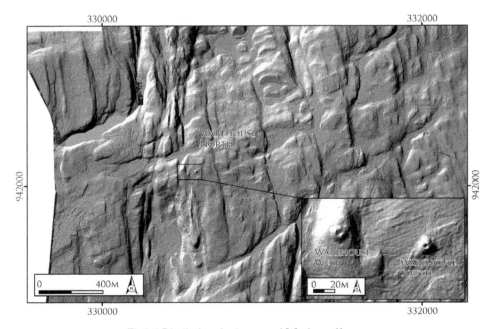

Fig 3.6 Distribution of cairns around Warehouse, Yarrows

of the antiquities of northern Europe and became involved in the systematic analysis, recording and protection of ancient monuments.

Rhind was a brilliant scholar whose work, and reputation, went far beyond the boundaries of Scotland. In his mid-twenties he excavated in the tombs at Thebes and worked with 50 men in the Valley of the Kings (Mowat 1912, 10). His writings on Egyptian tombs became standard works for students of the period. In 1858, Rhind bought a papyrus in Luxor, which proved to be the second-oldest Egyptian mathematical tract and can be dated to around 1650 BC in the Second Intermediate Period (Papyrus British Museum 10057 and 10058). This is a signally important text, both for Egyptologists and for students of the history of science. It is a wonderful document, written in hieratic and measuring 33 centimetres by 5 metres. Ahmes (i.e. Ahmose) the scribe of the papyrus, presents the papyrus as giving 'Accurate reckoning for inquiring into things, and the knowledge of all things, mysteries...all secrets'. There could be no more fitting footnote to the life of its discoverer and preserver, Alexander Henry Rhind.

The summer of 1858 was the last that Rhind spent at Sibster, which he had by then inherited. The remaining winters of his short life were divided between the south of France, Algiers and Madeira and he had a summer residence at Clifton, Bristol. He left England in 1862 and returned to the Nile where he 'carried out work systematically for 1,000 miles of the river's course' (letter written by Rhind, quoted in Mowat 1912, 11). He died in Zurich on 2 July 1863, aged 30, and was interred in the family burial ground at Wick, 11 days later.

Money from his estate was left to fund scholarships at Edinburgh University, and money from the Sibster estate was used to found a lectureship in archaeology (Omand 1989, 192). He also left a valuable library of some 1600 volumes (Mowat 1912, 11). But even in death he was adamant that he wanted the county's archaeology to remain central to Scottish prehistory. He left money to the Society of Antiquaries of Scotland with the intention that it was to be spent on research, primarily in Caithness, Sutherland and Ross-shire. These areas were chosen because he believed that the archaeology of the area was mostly unknown to the general student (Stuart 1868, 289): *plus ça change*. After visiting these areas himself, Stuart (*ibid.* 307) concurred with Rhind and argued that these counties should constitute the chief field of operations, providing that appropriate excavation techniques were employed. Just before the Christmas of 1866, the secretary to the Society of Antiquaries of Scotland

Fig 3.7 Alexander Rhind, one of the pioneer's of Caithness and Scottish archaeology (copyright Society Antiquaries of Scotland)

adopted the suggestions. Rhind's work and perseverance raised the county's profile within the Scottish archaeological fraternity for a time. Today he is commemorated in the annual Rhind Lectures, one of the most prestigious lecture series in Europe.

Rhind was a remarkable individual who worked with great energy despite very poor health. As Mowat (1912, 12) concluded, 'To his unruffled calmness we doubtless owe the lengthening of his days, and the many works crowded into little space'. Despite his obvious passion for the Middle East his home county was dear to his heart and he was aware of the richness of the area's archaeological remains and their importance to Scottish prehistory. He was particularly passionate about the area around the southern corner of the parish of Wick: the localities of Yarrows, Warehouse, Ulbster, Watenan, and Camster (see Stuart 1868, 292–3). At the age of 18, Rhind made a list of the remarkable monuments in these areas and, quite literally, put Caithness on the archaeological map (published posthumously by Stuart, 1868, 292–5). At that time archaeological records for Caithness were restricted to occasional references in the Old Statistical Account, the first of two reports (1790s and 1830) on life in Scotland during the agricultural and industrial revolutions. Both accounts were based on survey data provided by each parish minister and reported variously on wealth, poverty and class, climate, agriculture, population, education and schools, fishing and wildlife and the moral state of the people: no small undertaking.

It was over twenty years before the first series of Ordnance Survey maps for the county became available (Davidson & Henshall 1991, 6) and a few years more before Rhind investigated a number of these sites including the 'Pict's House' or broch at Kettleburn (Rhind 1853; 1854a). The excavation occupied several men for a period little short of three months. Not content with being the first person to explore a broch systematically, in the same year he also excavated the three cairns at Warehouse, and some others for good measure (Rhind 1854b). He was one of the first researchers to excavate archaeological sites in Caithness, and amongst the first anywhere to do so in a systematic way (Davidson & Henshall 1991, 6).

Rhind believed that systematic and careful examination of these remains would illustrate the feelings and condition of his ancestors (Stuart 1868, 289; see Rhind 1853, 1854a). Although Rhind uncovered features now viewed as typical of chambered cairns, including chambers, entrances passages, and so on, he does not seem to have been primarily interested in their structural minutiae; many of his plans and measurements are awry (Anderson 1866b, 444). Instead, Rhind's main purposes in excavating the cairns appear to have been the discovery of artefacts and the recovery of human skulls for comparative ethnological studies (then very fashionable) (Davidson & Henshall 1991, 6). In discussing the finds from Kettleburn broch, his interest in human remains prompted him to note that, 'scarcely less important than the articles which belong more particularly to the province of the Archaeologist, are the osteological remains' (Rhind 1854a, 268).

Here then, was the first systematic attempt to survey and excavate a group of monuments typical of northern Scotland. Stony mounds enticed an inquisitive genius to delve beneath their crusts in an attempt to characterise and understand the relics of the past. The recovery of human remains from the sites, albeit in a limited number, illustrated a connection with the dead – but in what way? And what were the defining structural characteristics of the cairns? Were they all circular in plan? Did they all have the same internal attributes? Were there any other secrets hidden within their bellies? Their dating was an equally vexed issue and in the absence of the written dedications and 'known' history, with which he was familiar in his Egyptian work, it was a question that must have seemed almost beyond answer. Rhind believed at first that the skill of the chambered-cairn builders 'had attained a step higher in the scale of civilisation that is indicated by the very rudest of our primeval remains' (Rhind 1854b, 107). He later concluded that the cairns belonged to the 'earliest Celtic population' and that they were probably Pictish (Stuart 1864, 10). As we write in 2014, we are following in the footsteps of Rhind by working with the local community to re-excavate the Warehouse cairns.

South Yarrows North and South

During his excavations at Warehouse, Rhind was aided by another illustrious scholar, Robert Shearer (Stuart 1868, 292). Shearer was born at Upper Thrumster in 1826, the eldest of James and Margaret Shearer's eleven children (Clark & Sellers 2005). In 1847, the family moved to Borrowston and subsequently moved to Ulbster House (now Ulbster Mains). The family was still there in 1871, though in the last years of his life Shearer appears to have moved to Thrumster Cottage (see Clark & Sellers 2005, 6). In 1861, James Shearer became a tenant farmer of Sir Tollemache Sinclair, Bart (*ibid.*). Robert Shearer progressed through the agricultural hierarchy of the time from farmer's son (1861 census) through to factor, or estate manager (1866, *John O'Groat Journal*), to estate agent (1871 census). He was a religious man and '… saw God's hand in the design and perfection of the natural world' (Clark & Sellers 2005, 12).

A series of more than 70 publications between 1859 and 1867, including some in the *John O'Groat Journal*, provide a glimpse into the life and ideals of Shearer. The articles were mainly concerned with the birds and mammals of Caithness and with Shearer's primary focus, the sea, coastline and lochs around the Thrumster/ Borrowston/ Ulbster area. His studies also extended beyond Caithness to Sutherland, Edinburgh and Cornwall. Like Rhind, Shearer was a thoughtful man, not one to rush to conclusions but impatient with errors in others (Clark & Sellers 2005, 13). This temperament is shown in his review of a contemporary of his, Samuel Laing, who was then excavating sites in and around Sinclair Bay (see later chapters). Evidently incensed by Laing's interpretations of the archaeology he was uncovering, Shearer prepared a paper for the Anthropological Society of London in 1866 which was published in the *John O'Groat Journal* on 14 June the same year. It is a vitriolic piece that questions the antiquity attributed by Laing to the monuments and artefacts he (Laing) was uncovering (Clark & Sellers 2005, 15). Samuel Laing is an equally interesting character and we will have cause to consider his career in Caithness later.

An accomplished naturalist, Shearer also had a deep interest in anthropology and archaeology. A year after Rhind died, the president of the Anthropological Society of London paused in Caithness on his way to Shetland. In anticipation of his visit, Shearer began excavating the chambered long cairn at South Yarrows South. This resulted in a

Fig 3.8 Joseph Anderson, a central figure in the study of Caithness prehistory

grant from the society to Shearer and Joseph Anderson for a 'thorough investigation of this hitherto unknown class of cairns' (Anderson 1866a, 234). This led to a fruitful relationship with Anderson around the mid to late 1860s. In 1872, the *John O'Groat Journal* noted that Shearer had been elected a corresponding member of the Society of Antiquaries of Scotland. He died three days later from a serious 'effusion of the brain'. He is buried in Thrumster cemetery.

Joseph Anderson (1832–1916) is the central figure in the study of the prehistory of Caithness (Fig. 3.8). Indeed, his work influenced the emergence of European prehistory. Born in Arbroath in 1832 he received his education at St Vigeans School. In 1856, he moved to Constantinople to teach English. This foreign sojourn did not last long and he returned to Scotland – to Wick in Caithness – four years later to become the editor of the *John O'Groat Journal*. During his stay in the county, which lasted less than a decade, he immersed himself in her archaeology. Although he left Caithness in 1869 to become the keeper of the National Museum of Antiquities of Scotland, Anderson remained actively involved in the study, recording, dissemination and interpretation of Caithness' prehistory (for a review of Anderson's life and career see Clarke 2002). Anderson was a well-respected individual and when Stuart was examining Caithness as part of a reconnaissance for the Society of Antiquaries of Scotland he availed himself of the opportunity to meet Anderson (Stuart 1868, 290).

As we shall see, Anderson excavated a number of sites and, more importantly, published his findings promptly in a number of lucid and stimulating papers. His authoritative discussions were remarkable at that stage of the study of British prehistory (see Davidson & Henshall 1991, 6–8, for a discussion of his contribution to the study of chambered cairns). Working with Shearer, Anderson augmented and expanded the work of Rhind and undertook an amazing spate of investigations. In 1865 alone, they investigated eight chambered cairns. They undertook new excavations at South Yarrows South; South Yarrows North; Ormiegill North; and Camster Round Cairn. They also returned to chambered cairns first investigated by Rhind. The following year they excavated three more chambered cairns: Camster Long; Cairn o'Get (Garrywhin) and Kenny's Cairn. Work was started, but subsequently abandoned, at Carn Righ chambered cairn because of its ruined state.

South Yarrows North and South cairns are less than 300 metres apart, lying to the west of the Loch of Yarrows (Fig. 3.9). Anderson's and Shearer's excavations were important for two reasons. First, they revealed a hitherto undiscovered type of cairn:

the long cairn. Second, they showed that these monuments could have been built, then used continuously or added to – or both – over lengthy periods. Both structures may have been composite monuments. South Yarrows North may comprise the core cairn and chamber, set within a long cairn, from which the core cairn and chamber are separated by an apparent gully. Whilst it is certainly possible that the two structural elements – core cairn and long cairn – were built at the same time, the divergence of the long axis of the chamber from the long axis of the cairn is sometimes adduced as proof that the long cairn is a separate and much later build than the core cairn. This inference is a non sequitur, that is it cannot be concluded that all contemporaneous builds on a given site must necessarily share a common axis. Traces of charcoal were discovered on an old ground surface along the axis of the cairn (Anderson 1866a, 237) at South Yarrows South, perhaps suggesting that there may have been pre-cairn activity in this area. At South Yarrows North a secondary cist was inserted into the round cairn chamber during the Bronze Age, a point to which we will return later.

Excavating only a few hundred metres from Rhind's Warehouse cairns, Shearer and Anderson uncovered a new class of monument and were able to elucidate the general structural characteristics of chambered cairns and their complex biographies. Anderson (1886, 234–5) observes about these excavations that:

> I was then a novice in the art of cairn exploration; and, like all novices, I thought only of the readiest method of cracking the nut to get at the kernel. It did not occur to me that there was anything to be done with the mere husk of the cairn beyond the discovery of the most direct method of access to its contents. Up to that time it had been the general opinion that the object of opening a cairn was simply to obtain its contents. In accordance with the usual opinion and practice, I cracked the nut, and found that it contained no kernel – or, in other words, that it held no relics that could be exhibited in a glass case.

Like many contemporaries, and like Rhind before him, Anderson was primarily spurred to excavate by the potential contents of the chambers, be they human remains or artefacts:

> Had the chamber been full of relics, the probability is that I should have been satisfied with the recovery of these, and the external structure of the cairn might have remained uninvestigated. It was, in fact the non-success of the search for relics that suggested the direction of the investigation to other results (Anderson 1886, 236).

Their disappointment with the poverty of the deposits in chambers serendipitously focussed their attention onto the structural complexities of the cairns themselves and the possibility that they had enjoyed very long periods of use.

> If the investigation of these examples of a very peculiar type of sepulchral structure has been singularly barren of results, as regards the associated relics which are the usual accompaniments of cairn burial, we have at least ascertained

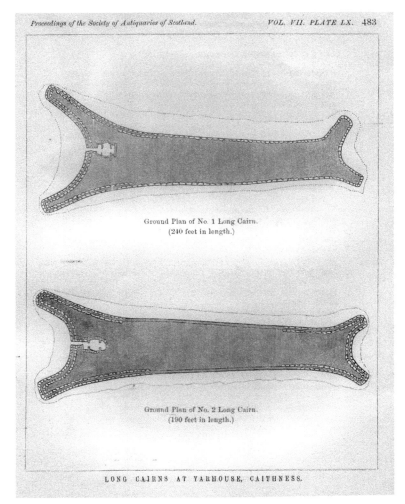

Proceedings of the Society of Antiquaries of Scotland. VOL. VII. PLATE LX. 483

Ground Plan of No. 1 Long Cairn.
(240 feet in length.)

Ground Plan of No. 2 Long Cairn.
(190 feet in length.)

LONG CAIRNS AT YARHOUSE, CAITHNESS.

Fig 3.9 South Yarrows North and South chambered cairns

a series of facts regarding the structure of the cairns themselves, which are full of significance (Anderson 1886, 243).

In spite of the fact that they had opened up around a sixth of the county's chambered cairns in the 1850s and 1860s, Anderson and Shearer were still no closer to knowing the dates of these structures. Today, we have access to a suite of scientific dating techniques but in the mid-nineteenth century, chronology building was a much tougher prospect. We have seen that, at least at some juncture, Rhind believed the cairns to be Pictish (Stuart 1864, 10), by which he meant Early Medieval (i.e. AD 400 to AD 1000). In the initial 1860s publications of his and Shearer's work Anderson was unclear about what date the chambered cairns were and acknowledged that it was premature to hazard an opinion (Anderson 1866b, 450). In 1868 he believed that the suggestion that the chambered cairns were the sepulchres of the broch builders had yet to be proved (Anderson 1868, 509). Like Rhind before him, he was keen to stress that those who erected the cairns were 'no despicable barbarians, but people possessed of considerable constructive skill, ingenuity, and resource' (ibid., 511). Eventually, two decades later, Anderson pinpointed the date of chambered cairns; by placing chambered cairns within their wider prehistoric framework Anderson was able to stress how different they were from Bronze Age and Iron Age burials and he placed them firmly within the Neolithic period (Anderson 1886, 229–60).

This groundbreaking work on chambered cairns by Rhind, Shearer and Anderson is characteristic of Caithness' archaeology, where large tracts of our current knowledge are based on the work of a small number of key individuals from the nineteenth century. At that time archaeology was not a profession; people did not make a living or a career out of archaeology and there were no university courses in the subject. The individuals who became involved in the subject were a motley crew. Victorian landowners were independently wealthy and could afford to spend their days 'doing archaeology' on their private estates. Barrow openings became a new form of entertainment. Others, of necessity, had to earn their livings and undertook fieldwork as and when they could. Different individuals not only had their own ways of excavating and recording, but also offered a variety of rationales for undertaking fieldwork. Some were only interested in the contents of the structures; others were equally as interested in the structures themselves. Although other contemporaries were happy just to uncover archaeological remains as an act of curiosity, Rhind and Anderson wished to characterise and analyse the emerging Caithness corpus within a wider geographical and intellectual framework. Archaeologies of Caithness had begun to emerge.

CAMSTER ROUND AND LONG

Archaeological excavation is a destructive process for some of the elements of our heritage. Once exposed, the characteristics and even the contents of some soil deposits begin to change; this is particularly true of waterlogged deposits, but is generally true of all soil types. Once it has been removed to reveal artefacts or structures, the original soil matrix cannot be restored. Our heritage is a finite, non-renewable and progressively wasting (due to natural changes) resource. This is why the discipline is, rightly, awash with legislation on and regulation of ancient monuments and artefacts, policies on planning and preservation of standing buildings, strict guidelines on standards and practices, and so on. Current practitioners comply with an ever-expanding suite of guidelines on archaeological practice.

But, of course, no regulation existed to guide Rhind, Anderson, Shearer and their contemporaries. Not all artefacts were kept for the nation's enjoyment, as is now the norm in Scotland. Although he later became the Keeper of the National Museum of Antiquities of Scotland, Anderson did not seem especially interested in the curation of artefacts. In certain cases, particularly with his Neolithic excavations, he did not manage to ensure the survival of many finds (Clarke 2002, 7). Similarly, most of

Fig 3.10 Camster Round cairn

Fig 3.11 Camster Long cairn

the artefacts and human remains uncovered by Rhind during his chambered-cairn excavations cannot now be found.

As well as excavating at Warehouse and Yarrows, Joseph Anderson also excavated the nearby long cairn and round cairn at Camster. These cairns also contributed to his elucidation of the structural characteristics and dating of chambered cairns. They are breathtaking sites, well worth a visit. In the RCAHMS 1911 Inventory (RCAHMS 1911, 184), Curle noted that Camster Round Cairn 'is the finest example of an excavated chambered cairn in the county, if not in Scotland'. Today, the site is undoubtedly impressive and presents itself as a large circular stone cairn with fragments of its façade still surviving (Fig. 3.10). Only a few hundred metres away is Camster Long Cairn, an equally impressive spectacle (Fig. 3.11). If there were an award for the most impressive site in Caithness, Camster Long Cairn would certainly come out near the top of everyone's list. Today, it stands proud in the landscape as an impressive, but much reduced, stony mound covering two chambers, many of the structural characteristics of which are clearly visible, such as passages, chambers and horned facades.

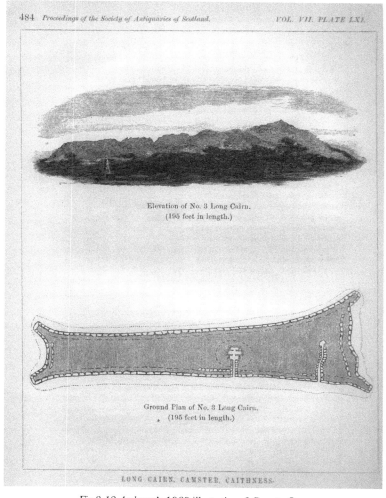

Fig 3.12 Anderson's 1868 illustration of Camster Long

But the Camster cairns have not always looked like that. Anderson's 1868 illustration of Camster Long portrays the site as a rugged configuration, its jagged profile in stark contrast to the sleek contour one admires today (Fig 3.12). The monument has deteriorated since Anderson's excavation, partly as a result of his work and the work of the more recent re-excavations, but also because of natural changes and probably the intermittent and continued removal of stone from the cairns. When Curle visited the site in 1910, he found that one of the passages was blocked and a chamber had suffered a minor collapse on the south-west side (RCAHMS 1911, 183). Archaeology is, as we have noted, a destructive process. When monuments are buried under soil and as a result of their own collapse, an environmental balance with the soils in which they lie develops. Decomposition may continue, at a reduced rate, but usually some approximate equilibrium is reached. Then, when they are dug up, and subsequently revealed to the public, that equilibrium is disturbed and may deteriorate dramatically. This is a common feature, even on World Heritage Sites, where the losses owing to natural processes are amplified by the impacts of tourism. The heritage legislation and regulation discussed above is designed to prevent or limit the loss of the historic fabric of our monuments and sites through the prevention of unhelpful interventions by humans. It does absolutely nothing to protect monuments from the gradual, and sometimes not so gradual, depredations of time and nature.

State intervention, which includes maintaining and presenting sites for the visitor, has resulted in exemplary care of monuments by national agencies such as Historic Scotland or the National Trust, and by local councils and voluntary groups (see Archaeology Scotland's Adopt-a-Monument scheme for examples).

Since the mid-twentieth century, aspects of fieldwork have become bound up with the emergence of 'public archaeology' and the desire to exhibit the remains of the more spectacular of these structures to the public at large (Armit 2003, 22). For the first time, state funds have been made available for the excavation and display of archaeological monuments, sometimes in partnership with landowners and other benefactors. Thus, it is now possible to visit some splendid archaeological sites across Scotland including the Neolithic village of Skara Brae; the broch village at Gurness, on Orkney; and the broch and Viking settlement at Jarlshof, on Shetland. This 'democratisation' of archaeological presentation for the benefit of a wider public has set a trend which continues to this date, but which has, inevitably come with some unintended consequences.

The carefully manicured lawns on which state-managed or National Trust monuments are displayed are of course an artefact of the twenty-first century: the builders of these structures certainly never saw them like that. Most monuments are palimpsests that include evidence for many periods and have seen much redevelopment over time. Since professional archaeologists and civil servants generally display little faith in the intelligence of the public, the 'distractions' of multi-period structures have been traditionally reduced to the artificial simplicity of a single period. Simpler it may be, but our heritage it is not. Nor is this iniquity the special reserve of archaeologists; conservation architects often construct greater simplifications, as the castles at Stirling and Edinburgh now attest: their public presentations focus on a single period in each case and their manifest chronological complexity is largely ignored.

Fig 3.13 The broch complex at Gurness, Orkney (copyright Graeme Cavers)

The broch complex at Gurness, Orkney, is a good example of an early attempt to present to the public something of the chronological complexity of the monument, but it is arguably still a practice of simplification (Fig. 3.13). Robert Rendall first explored the site on a very small scale in 1929. Before the end of July that year, J. S. Richardson – then inspector of Ancient Monuments for Scotland – had seen the exploratory pit. Equipped with a donation from T. B. Macaulay, Richardson asked the Society of Antiquaries of Scotland to conduct more excavations. The council of the society asked Hewat Craw to act on their behalf and in 1930 excavations began, and continued for ten seasons. The importance of the site was recognised and it was placed under state guardianship in 1931 (see Hedges 1987, 1–14).

It is significant that what we would now term the 'excavation strategy' was heavily influenced, indeed driven, by a desire to consolidate the structures for public display:

> There was from the beginning a constant bias in excavation towards structures, stripped of unnecessary adhesions, which could be consolidated and displayed. This was because, whether the Society of Antiquaries or H M o W were the organising body, display was one of the primary and explicit objectives of the exercise. Every year there was not only excavation by a supervisor and his workmen but also consolidation and reconstruction first by contractors and then by a Ministry foreman and hands; the estimates and grants were channelled through the Architects' Department mainly because of the organisational structure current, though in giving a grant, excavation and reconstruction were seen as two aspects of the same project (Hedges 1987, 213).

Following Craw's death in 1933, Richardson devolved work to Balfour, Yeoman, Craig-Brown and Tulloch. During this period, 'all the structures outside the broch were tidied up for display' and after 'a decade and a half of neglect [following the War] reconsolidation work recommenced, the result being the monument as it is known today' (Hedges 1987, 2).

This is not the place for a detailed review of the site, which has in any event already been done by others (Hedges 1987; MacKie 1994; 2002, 227–32), but we should pause and consider how the rationale and methods behind the work created the monument and affected the visitor's experience of it.

It is clear that recording of stratigraphy was of secondary concern. The primary levels of the broch, the excavation of which would now assume a central role in the research design of a comparable project, were left largely untouched because of a reluctance to remove later features that it was felt would have been pleasing to the public. MacKie (2002, 228) notes that this is one of the more unfortunate aspects of the work. The desire for an architecturally coherent monument, for public display, resulted in the removal of whole structures to other parts of the site. An entire Pictish building was removed from immediately outside the broch and reconstructed a short distance away. This venture facilitated the display of a lower set of comparable structures juxtaposed with the broch and its defences. Indeed, this removal and resiting, stone by stone, of later first millennium AD structures was one of the achievements of which the workers were most proud (Hedges 1987, 13).

As it stands today, Gurness is undoubtedly a visually impressive site. Whilst there are references to the original positions of, for example, the Pictish structures, the texts and guidebooks are largely dominated by explanations of the definition, date and function of the broch, as it is now presented. At Gurness, concern with presenting a simple and pristine site as a basis for a simple and pristine narrative resulted in the sculpting of the site and the removal of evidence for architectural and archaeological relationships. And Gurness is not atypical of the handling of archaeological sites in the twentieth century.

The vast majority of the prehistoric monuments in Caithness that are under state ownership, or state guardianship, are chambered cairns, many of which were excavated by Anderson. We have seen that in 1910 Camster Long was deteriorating. The site was re-excavated in 1967 and 1968 by P. R. Ritchie, for what was then the Ministry of Public Buildings and Works (MoPBW). Ritchie's work was confined to minor excavations at the entrances to both passages, the removal of collapsed roofing and some consolidation work (Masters 1997, 127). In 1971, John X. W. P. Corcoran was invited by the Department of the Environment to undertake a major programme of excavation. Corcoran, an exemplary archaeological fieldworker, excavated for three seasons. Following Corcoran's death, L. J. Masters completed the excavation between 1976 and 1980.

This sequence of excavations led to a better understanding and questioning of the multi-period use of these sites and excavation of the long cairn enabled the study of its construction. But, in contrast to Anderson's approach, the works of Ritchie, Corcoran and Masters were all 'geared towards a final situation where the public would have safe access to the cairn' which of course required 'a great deal of restoration work' (Masters 1997, 129). Lionel Masters (1997, 173–4) summarises the rationale for restoration:

There can be no doubt that the visitor today will see in Camster Long a monument which is strikingly impressive. The change from a tumbled mass of stones with vegetation growing up the edges to, it is hoped, a pristine monument complete with forecourts, revetments and chambers, coupled with a visually distinctive hummocky cairn profile, now forms a dramatic feature rising out of the bleak moorland. … The writer is convinced of the wisdom of the decision, by MoPBW and its successors, to restore the external appearance of the cairn. The practice of conserving only the remains of those features surviving *in situ* would have led, at Camster, to a visual appearance more likely to confuse than instruct the visitor.

This 'tidying up' and desire for a 'pristine' monument – fingerprints of state intervention – is arguably appropriate for some aspects of archaeology, but not for all. We will return to this issue later when we consider the work of Sir Francis Tress Barry and the brochs he excavated. But it is worth raising here the importance of understanding what we may term the 'investigation biography' of any archaeological monument when presenting the site to the public.

In our view, a visitor should be able to engage in an interpretational dialogue with a monument and our role as archaeologists is to present the conflicting theories and explain the – admittedly usually ambiguous – evidence from the monument and its potential relevance to the theories in play. We do not support the practice of simplifying either the physical monuments or their interpretations to suit some imagined consensus position. Perversely, some archaeological 'simplifications' of monuments have created chimera that confuse, mislead or complicate the situation without really helping the lay visitor. We acknowledge that the presentation of information on sites and monuments is a difficult problem and one that probably has no 'right' answer; nonetheless, we contend that superficial, simplistic presentations are not the answer.

With heritage sites and monuments, we take on a stewardship role, managing them now so that this and future generations can explore their human patrimony. We should embrace a presumption against undertaking works that are not necessary for the conservation of the cultural value of the monuments, regardless of whether or not this makes them more accessible, literally or metaphorically, to the wider public. Surely it would be better to improve the education of the public, to enable them to understand their monumental inheritance, than to degrade that inheritance to accommodate their apparently limited comprehension. Sadly, the monuments that have suffered most from the interpreters and presenters are probably the best examples of their types. We could look upon these as sacrificial lambs and further accommodate, with regard to such monuments, the urge of the interpreters and presenters to make them all more accessible to the inarticulate and the apparently barely educated (the latter is not our judgement but the implied judgement of the simplifiers).

Cultural tourism has been embraced by the social engineers amongst us, in part to make accessible to everybody in society the experience of our shared cultural inheritance, which was previously available only to the very wealthy and the highly educated (often the same group). Considering the vandalism of the few who made the 'grand tour', it is hard to see why they have been selected as worthy of emulation. It is not unusual nowadays to encounter, at great cultural sites, members of the public who have no interest whatsoever in what they are viewing. 'Experience bagging' is not exceptionable: it provides a happy diversion in many modern lives and may inspire a deeper interest in some; we do not object to it, but we do very strongly object to the gratification of such transient interests via the ill-considered modification of the monuments that form the greater part of humanity's cultural inheritance. We object even more to such modifications when they are geared towards revenue generation at popular sites and monuments. For example, there can be no justification for the building of new shops on ancient monuments or for the extensive modifications needed to insert restaurants into ancient buildings. These are the acts of vandals, regardless of how fashionable or how sympathetic the new architecture may be.

This may seem curmudgeonly, but it is founded on the simple point that no generation should assume the right to modify our heritage either for financial gain or in pursuit of some social principle, even one as laudable as securing access for all to our shared heritage. We support wholeheartedly the idea of extending such access, but never at the expense of the heritage to which the access is being secured. We simply do not have the right to do this. Tarting up old ruins may be a beautician's ambition but it should form no part of a heritage professional's concern, and in a better informed world it would not get public support either.

Today, Camster Long stands proud in the landscape and many visitors to the site would, quite understandably, presume that the site had always been that way. There is no information saying otherwise. But Camster Long was investigated by different individuals with a variety of rationales, including simple interest; recovery of human remains and artefacts; information on structural complexity; restoration; consolidation; and public presentation. Each investigation modified the monument and, in so doing, rescripted the monument's apparent biography. Camster Long looked different before Anderson set to work. Curle would have seen a completely different structure from that which Anderson first investigated a quarter of a century earlier. A further half century of cumulative natural and anthropic change altered this in turn before the investigations of Ritchie, Corcoran and Masters.

Referring to the experiences of visitors from all over the world at Camster Long, Masters (1997, 175) informs us that there were varying perceptions of how much of the cairn was original.

> This, it must be confessed, ranged from a very few visitors who thought that the fibreglass domes were part of the original structure, to those who would have liked some indication of what was original and what was modern restoration in such features as the revetments and façades. Given the amount of reconstruction, rebuilding and consolidation at Camster Long, this would be difficult to achieve. There might have been a case for distinguishing in some way – perhaps by means of a slate course – original from restored revetments and chamber walls. This would not have detracted from the visual appearance and, suitably indicated, would have satisfied those visitors who considered it important.

Several national and international conservation charters now exist which try to set out best practice for the conservation of heritage places. The problem set out by Masters above is addressed in these charters because it is a matter of fundamental principle that changes to a heritage asset should be the minimum necessary, and should be reversible and identifiable. Masters referred to the possibility of using a layer of slates within rebuilt walls to distinguish the new from the old; this has been done on many sites and is indeed helpful. However, during our experimental work at Spittal we noted that fallen stones form patterns of collapse, from which it is sometimes possible to deduce the form of the structure from which they fell. This in turn has a bearing on the cairns' taphonomy – that is, the process by which deposits are formed – which in this case concern accumulations formed in and around the cairns and deposits that incorporate artefacts, and so on. Much of the material recovered from the excavation of chambered cairns is intermixed with stone from episodes of collapse and yet all of the material is treated as indicative of the primary use of the monument. We really need to know much more about how monuments decay to the forms in which we find them, not least how quickly they begin to disintegrate following their completion. If the reinstatement of materials is a requirement for a given monument and consistent with the conservation of its cultural value, we really need to do more than insert a layer of slates. Even the reinstated parts of a conserved monument will, in time, become parts of the next episodes of collapse of the structure. Then they will become part of the next deposit-forming process. If we had some way to identify uniquely where each introduced stone came from, or even where each layer, or course, of stones had come from in the reconstruction, we would learn far more about the real-world vectors of instability, decay and collapse, and about the taphonomic process by which the deposits in and around the monument were formed, than we can learn from simple experimentation. The latter can pose and explore research questions drawn from real-world observations, but we need real-world examples to demonstrate the validity, or invalidity, of the results of our necessarily limited and simple experiments. In reality, each episode of reconstruction for conservation reasons could also become a long-term experiment of immense value to heritage management.

We must anticipate that future interventions in heritage monuments will be guided by conservation planning and that nothing will be done to a monument that cannot be undone and that is not clearly identifiable as a modern modification.

4. CIST BURIALS OF THE BRONZE AGE

WAREHOUSE 5, GARRYWHIN, WARTH HILL AND ACHAROLE

In the old three-age system, the Stone Age gives way to the Bronze Age, which in turn gives way to the Iron Age in an imagined onward and upward march to increasing technical complexity and competence. Whilst this is still a useful general scheme, it has become clear that the transitions from one of these periods to another can be complex, protracted and uneven in time and space. The transition from the Neolithic (the 'New Stone Age') to the Bronze Age is one such transition.

Whilst investigating the chambered cairns at Warehouse, Rhind's attention was drawn to another stony mound, Warehouse 5, which was subsequently excavated by Sinclair. He found the stone cairn to be of an entirely different structure from those in the immediate neighbourhood: it was simply a huge pile of stones raised over a *kistvaen* (or cist) that was composed of massive slabs (the term 'cist' simply means 'box'). The cist contained the skull and bones of a human skeleton lying on a quantity of beach gravel (RCAHMS 1911, 175, no. 551; Davidson & Henshall 1991, 156, no. 66). Later, Joseph Anderson (1868, 502) recorded that the cairn contained a bronze dagger or spearhead, which is now believed to be an Early Bronze Age dagger or knife (Coles 1969, 90). Interest in the Caithness Bronze Age had begun.

Spurred on by Rhind's work, Anderson was drawn to another untouched stone mound at Garrywhin, where excavation revealed a cist containing a bowl-shaped urn, two flint flakes and the enamel crowns from human molars (Fig. 4.1; Anderson 1868, 503; 1886, 126–8). Anderson then turned his attention to another cairn at Warth Hill, Canisbay. Prior to his work, a flagstone cist containing a skeleton had been exposed in one side of the cairn. Convinced that this was not the original interment, Anderson opened the centre of the cairn and found another cist in which traces of a skeleton were noted. Despite the absence of artefacts from the cist, Anderson (1872, 294) had little doubt that the cairn was prehistoric. The general characteristics of the structure and the discovery in 1925 of a Late Bronze Age socketed axehead below Warth Hill (discussed in a later chapter) lent credibility to his suggestion. A few decades later Robert Sutherland, excavating for gravel at Acharole, West Watten, discovered yet another cist, which contained a burial and a Beaker pot (Bryce 1905). The skeleton, which lay in a contracted position, was sent to Sir Francis Tress Barry for comment and he concluded that the skeleton was 'that of a male in the early part of adult life' (*ibid.* 421). As we have seen, John Nicolson drew the excavated remains in a series of sketches and paintings, which act as archaeological sections through the site (Fig. 1.7). In this case, he appears to depict the cist sitting within a grass-covered gravel mound (see also Bryce 1905, 418–9).

The Bronze Age burial rite based on single inhumations under small mounds or cairns – or unmarked by either – differs from the multiple burials in monumental architecture of the preceding Neolithic period discussed in

Fig 4.1 The cist burial at Garrywhin

the earlier chapter. Cist burials were carried out in a variety of forms: some contained inhumations, possibly accompanied by pottery vessels, jet necklaces, bronze objects, and so on; some held cremations contained in large pottery urns. The differences in burial practices and material cultures between the Neolithic and the Bronze Age obviously indicated a significant cultural shift as well as the obvious technological advance. Perhaps by providing objects of value with very long shelf lives, the use of copper and bronze allowed the accumulation of wealth in ways not previously possible. Cattle, sheep or bags of wheat can only be accumulated for as long as there is carrying capacity in terms of land and in any event, they have finite lifetimes. Interments in cist burials vary over a wide range in terms of status: some of the dead were clearly very rich, others less so; is it possible then that wealth accumulation facilitated the emergence of social castes?

In addition, the mobility of Bronze Age people within the landscape is only just beginning to be revealed. Recent work on radiometric trace element analyses indicates that a cist burial near Stonehenge contained the remains of a man who had spent his childhood in Switzerland. Similar cases have been noted elsewhere, for example in Bavaria (Price *et al.* 1998, 405). Studies now under way on Beaker burials from Yorkshire also point to the possible wide-scale regional migration of individuals. Regrettably, we have no published accounts of comparable work on human remains from Neolithic sites. We assume, for now, that physical and social mobility, as well as the clearer social differentiation evidenced in cist burials, would have made Bronze Age society quite different from Neolithic society, accepting that our ability to define either is quite limited.

CRAIG-NA-FEICH, ACHAVANICH

In 1987, a contractor called William Ganson dug for rock to use in road improvements at Craig-na-Feich near Achavanich. Below the bucket of his digger he noticed a skull peeping out from a hole in the rock. The skeleton of a young woman aged between 18 and 22, was buried in a crouched position in a cist. She was accompanied by three small pieces of flint and a Beaker pot. The burial was around 4000 years old. Analysis of the residue in the pot suggested that it had contained a cereal-based mixture flavoured with honey, meadowsweet, bramble and wood sage. The analyst concluded from this that, 'there are here multiple bases for fermentation, and that the outcome of collecting them would be an alcoholic hotchpotch'. As the Highland Council leaflet designated to the Achavanich cist burial stated at the time, 'This then, could have been the earliest known alcohol from Caithness!' In addition, other potential beers have been found in Beaker pottery from cist burials.

It was suggested in the 1970s that the remarkable spread of Beaker pottery (from the Atlas Mountains to Scandinavia, and from Ireland to Poland, in a period of less than two centuries) could only be explained in terms of a religious or cult expansion. This quickly lost favour but the association of so many Beakers with fermented drinks does make one wonder whether we abandoned it too quickly (Scott 1977). Certainly, no other credible explanation has been offered for the spread of Beakers throughout mainland Europe.

The Achavanich burial was unusual in that it had been cut into solid rock. It was also not, as far as we can tell, covered with a cairn or mound. This too is unusual, as most excavated burials had associated cairns. Burial cairns and mounds built *de novo* in the Bronze Age may be small structures covering single burials or large, sometimes multi-period, structures covering several cists. The latter are sometimes called multiple-cist cairns or cemetery cairns. Whilst some Bronze Age cairns are set on or close to the skyline, many are set in inconspicuous locations and therefore we cannot accept the general view that these cairns were intended to dominate the surrounding landscape. Indeed the diversity of chosen locations rather suggests that personal factors, such as freedom of access to specific locations or the affection of the deceased for particular spots in the landscape, are as likely to have motivated the choice of burial site as any more profound cosmological consideration.

It is also fairly common to find a Bronze Age cist inserted into the cairn or chamber of a Neolithic chambered cairn or, for that matter, to find a Bronze Age burial without an enclosing cist but within a chambered cairn. Indeed, cists have been found in significant numbers as secondary insertions into clearance cairns, which are heaps of stone piled up to clear areas of land for grazing or cultivation (e.g. Barber 1997, 87–93). Let us take a closer look at this phenomenon.

REUSE OF NEOLITHIC MONUMENTS

There are many antiquarian references to finds of cists near or on chambered cairns, although, again, many are difficult to date. These include Shean Stemster and Sinclair's Shean, Stemster. The place-name element 'shean' could be a transliteration of the modern Gaelic 'sean', meaning 'old', but it is far more likely to relate to the term 'sithean', meaning 'fairy mound' or 'fairy place'. In fact, the name of a Caithness chambered cairn known as 'Na Tri Sithean' sounds closer to a Celtic place name.

Shean Stemster was opened by Sir Francis Tress Barry during the 1890s and records of his work include annotated plans and watercolours by Nicolson. One of Nicolson's watercolours shows a crouched inhumation within a cist on the floor of the antechamber. Records also suggest that a short cist containing a crouched inhumation was found at Sinclair's chambered cairn in about 1880. Similarly, during excavations of the chambered cairn at Lower Dounreay, Arthur Edwards came upon a secondary burial, the cairn stones of the fallen roof utilised as material for the long cist in which to place the body. The cist contained the extended inhumation of a male, aged 20 to 25 (Low in Edwards 1929). He was covered with beach shingle, amongst which fragments of a Beaker urn were found (Edwards 1929, 141–2). Although Davidson & Henshall (1991, 68, 126) suggested that the burial may be Iron Age or possibly Norse in date, and that the Beaker fragments were displaced, this need not be the case. Sometime before 1871, several cists were found in the top of the chambered cairn at Cnoc na Ciste, Sordale Hill (Davidson & Henshall 1991, 109). Two decades later, farmers removed a heavy lintel and came upon a niche in the wall that was protected in front by a light slab, behind which was a food vessel. The intact vessel was found in what may have been a cist at the side of the passage (Davidson & Henshall (1991, 77). According to the ONB (Old Name Book), a stone coffin containing human remains and a pot was found in the chambered Cairn of Heathercro in 1871, although it is uncertain whether the 'coffin' was a cist or part of the chamber investigated by Barry during the 1890s. Of course, it could have been both! Digging into a stone cairn is not easy and if the Early Bronze Age digger had encountered the side slabs of the chamber or passage, these might have automatically been used to create the side slabs of a new cist.

At South Yarrows North, a Bronze Age short cist was inserted into the antechamber of the chambered cairn. Contained in the filling of 'blackened clay' were decayed, cremated bones and a broken, coarse string-impressed pot, either a late Beaker vessel or a food container (now lost), and seventy lignite beads from a single-string jet necklace, still lying as they had been threaded (see Davidson & Henshall 1991, 77, 141).

There may be even more evidence for Bronze Age burials in and around chambered cairns. During excavations at Tulloch of Assery chambered cairn, a crouched burial of an adult – aged around 20, and probably a male – was uncovered in the centre of the main chamber, lying on large slabs argued to be collapsed roofing. A cremation deposit was also inserted into slip from the chambered cairn at Tulach an t'Sionnaich: the burials were clearly secondary to the main use of the chambered cairn. The cremation had been enclosed in a container which Corcoran (1966, 12) believed to be: 'an urn in the Bronze Age tradition', though reanalysis suggests that the pot may be a Beaker (A. Sheridan pers. comm.). A thumb-nail scraper of flint and two unworked flint fragments were found inside the deposit.

Returning to Shean Stemster, remains of a second inhumation and pieces of pot were found in the debris near the top of the cairn. At Camster Round, broken bones from the upper parts of two skeletons were recovered 'not on the floor but amongst the stones above it' (Anderson 1866b, 450). Although these may date to the sealing of the chamber and passages (Davidson & Henshall 1991, 66), they need not date to the Neolithic. The same is true of the bones from M'Cole's Castle.

Although the evidence is far from ideal there is, we believe, a good case for suggesting that Bronze Age groups and individuals chose to bury their dead within the presumably eroding, but still prominent, structures of their ancestors. This suggestion is supported by other evidence for Bronze Age activity on and around chambered cairns. Beakers are known from Lower Dounreay and Tulach an T'Sionnaich, and pottery from other chambered cairns, for example Kenny's Cairn, may also be Bronze Age in date (Davidson & Henshall 1991, 76). The battleaxe from Breckigoe chambered cairn, a prestige object often found with earlier Bronze Age graves (see Davidson & Henshall 1991, 77), only adds to the growing corpus.

Where opportunity presented itself, it is clear that Bronze Age burials were inserted into Neolithic chambered cairns. In general, the evidence suggests that the chambered cairns were already ruinous when the Bronze Age burials were inserted, a process that often did further damage to the chambered cairn. These secondary burials in chambered cairns cannot, therefore, be interpreted as a continuation of Neolithic practices. Rather, they imply that the chambered cairns, though ruinous, were still venerated by the local communities. We need not doubt that convenience also played a part in the process, but it is unlikely to have been the only motivating factor. Perhaps the Early Bronze Age burials in chambered cairns can be compared with Christian burials taking place in and about the ruins of early church sites, a practice which continues to this day. Perhaps those who undertook the Early Bronze Age burials shared our modern sense that some places are appropriate places for burial, consecrated to the dead or associated with burial by long tradition. We have stood recently in Christian graveyards observing the burial of atheists by atheists, with all, no doubt, taking sincere comfort from the hallowed context of the burial. The death of others occasions in us an existential dread of death and a renewal of fear for our rediscovered mortality that amplifies our sense of loss and compounds our grief. These emotions, we suggest, are what sanctify the experience of death and the locus of burial, not the ponderous musings of clergymen or some subtlety of landform, with or without ruins.

5. STONE ROWS, CIRCLES AND BENDS

Visitors to the north of mainland Scotland should make an effort to see some of the area's stone rows because there is nothing like them elsewhere in Britain. One would have to travel to Brittany to encounter equivalent monuments, albeit on a much larger scale. In their Caithness expression, these remarkable monuments consist of parallel or radiating rows of small standing stones: up to a hundred individual stones with few, if any, more than 50 centimetres high. In the absence of more prosaic explanations, it has long been suggested that these stone rows form some sort of astronomical observatory or calendrical device, although the latter is also an astronomical instrument of sorts.

Sir Henry Dryden surveyed some of these sites but the first precise surveys were undertaken by Professor Alexander Thom, who worked extensively on the archaeoastronomy of many monuments in the British Isles and Brittany. Since his time, other rows have been found and been studied by local Caithnessian, Lesley Myatt. A graduate of London University and a trained chartered electrical engineer, Lesley was also head of the Engineering and Building Department at Thurso Technical College. He has lived in Caithness for over forty years and during this time has immersed himself in the county's archaeology, particularly stone settings; Thom's work attracted Lesley to the study of these and he has visited and surveyed many of them over the last 40 years. Lesley has published a series of articles and books on the subject (Myatt; 1988; 1992; 2003) and much of what follows is drawn from his wonderful syntheses. For brilliant descriptions of the known monuments please see his 1988 and 2003 publications.

Over 20 stone rows are known from the county, of which Mid-Clyth is arguably the most impressive (Fig. 5.1). The greatest concentrations lie in the areas of Yarrows and Watenan (Myatt 1988, 278–81, Fig. 12.2; 2003, 7, 31–4, Fig. 18). The largest setting in that area is at Garrywhin, with other nearby examples at Loch Watenan, Watenan and Broughwhin. The paucity of excavations, the absence of dating evidence and the lack of associated artefacts mean that we have no direct evidence for the date/s of these stone settings. A Bronze Age date is generally suggested, but there is no substantive basis for this yet published. Astronomical theorising apart (Thom 1971; see also Myatt 1988, 317–18), speculation on their functions includes a link with 'socio-sepulchral customs' (Burl 1976, 156), in other words some form of ritual function. The truth is

Fig 5.1 Hill o' Many Stanes

that we have no more direct evidence for their functions than we have for their dates and in this instance your opinion is as good as any archaeologist's.

The recent excavation of a set of stone rows at Battle Moss, Yarrows, is beginning to shed new light on these monuments. Although no diagnostic finds or datable materials were recovered from secure contexts, the excavators assert that the monument may have been built in segments or phases over an unknown period of time (Baines, Brophy & Pannett 2003, 95). Recent work on the stone rows of Le Manio, Carnac, Brittany and the Megalithic chamber at Kerburg, Loire Atlantique has revealed that the standing stones, up to 3 metres high, were quarried in the immediate locality from low, rounded, granite tors (Mens 2008, 25–36). The stones have been conceptually 'refitted' to determine the order of quarrying and of erection. No direct evidence for the overall rate of erection was established but a detailed analysis of the *chaîne opératoire* (i.e. the chain or sequence of operations) has been possible, with interesting and exciting results.

Some of the Battle Moss stones appear misaligned: they are set at, or close to, right angles to the line of the stone row in which they occur. In the past it has been assumed that this was to the result of soil movement, but excavations suggest that this may not have been the case and that the stones had been deliberately set as we now find them. Recent scholars argue that many of these 'misaligned' stones are referencing, if not actually pointing to, monuments already present in the landscape prior to the construction of the stone rows, particularly Neolithic chambered cairns. However, examination of the 'referencing' on the ground by the current authors does little to instil confidence in this conclusion because of the lack of any consistency or accuracy in the selection of the putative sight lines.

Some stone rows within the Yarrows and Watenan areas appear to have been associated, perhaps even aligned, with cairns that have cist burials. The aforementioned cist cairn at Garrywhin, for example, sits at the apex of the adjacent stone row, described by Anderson (1886, 126) as a series of rows of grey slabs, like the headstones of a country churchyard (Fig. 4.1). On the other side of the valley there is a similar cairn juxtaposed with stone rows (Anderson 1868, 503–4). A similar arrangement of cairn and stone row has been noted at Camster (Anderson 1868, 503; 1886, 129). Of course we must accept that there cannot be a logical objection to the idea that the stone rows came first and the cairns second, in reverse of the preferred ordering of events: rather, we make this point to highlight the desperate weakness of these speculations.

It has long been argued that ceremonial centres originated in the Bronze Age and involved cist burials, stone rows or stone circles, and other monuments. More recently, it has been suggested that the landscape within which the monuments were set formed an integral part of the ceremonial setting. Recent writers have also placed great emphasis on the idea of the monument as a manifestation of memory; perhaps they have not fully understood the meaning of the term 'monument', which has always enshrined this concept.

During the Neolithic, the chambered cairns were monumental structures that embodied some expression of local cultural values. It is by no means clear that the chambered cairns were built as tombs; they can equally well be viewed as temples in which, over time, certain remains came to be interred. The fact that at least some of these interments post-dated the construction of the monument by a long way should serve as a caution against making the simplistic assumption that chambered cairns are communal ossuaries. The physical remains of the cairns, the open access to the chambers and the periodic reuse of the monuments (see above) indicate a role that could be seen to indicate continuity of engagement. Scholars postulate that ceremonies were conducted in the vicinity of the chambered cairns, again in the absence of direct evidence. Some argue that the continuity of use and strong ceremonial involvement with the monument would have established or renewed social knowledge, or social values, or power and social hierarchy, or some other social value. This is, from the extant evidence, unknowable but not inherently improbable.

During the Bronze Age, the burial rite became focussed on the individual, and single grave burials predominate. Furthermore, once the cist was sealed, there is no indication that it was to be opened again and it appears that the intention was for it to remain hidden from view. As we have seen, the location of some cists was marked with a cairn or mound, some of which were – or approached a scale that could be described as – monumental. For other Bronze Age burials, there may have been alternative grave markers, possibly made from organic materials that have since decayed, or the areas within which the burials were deposited may have been identifiable to Bronze Age peoples from such markers. In general, evidence for these markers did not survive and we therefore do not know whether they were in fact used, but Nicolson may have recorded such a connection in his depiction of the cist burial at Acharole (Fig. 1.7).

There, the cist clearly sat beside a standing stone, a prominent marker and reminder in the landscape.

It has been widely suggested that rites or ceremonies were acted out within the immediate environs of the burials and again this is likely, even if we rarely or never see archaeological evidence for it. In the case of cremations, there would automatically have been some theatricality associated with burning the body and gathering the remains for the final burial. Work done in Orkney by Jane Downes seems to show that the burning of the body regularly took place near the cist and it is possible that further information will be gleaned by further studies of this type.

CIRCLES AND BENDS

In starting any enterprise – a book, a rock band, a restaurant, whatever – its naming is often amongst the first considerations. When one of us (JB) was commissioned to draft a heritage developmental plan for the county's archaeology some years ago, we settled on the title 'River of Stone'. This was chosen because the heritage of Caithness is preserved in its wonderful native building stone and the stone structures of the county flow from the remote past to our own times in a continuous river of human endeavour.

Like many areas of Britain, Ireland and Europe the tradition of erecting standing stones in various forms flourished in Caithness. We have already encountered the stone rows and some standing stones and noted the uncertainty of their dating. Many are attributed to the Bronze Age (Anderson 1886; Thom, Thom & Burl 1990, 419) but we have noted the vanishingly small foundations to that attribution. Stone circles are the most monumental examples of orthostatic (made from upright stones) structures and although there are probably more stone circles than you might think, it is still difficult to give a precise number: although Myatt (2003, 23–27) gives a useful summary. If you live in the parishes of Thurso, Olrig, Dunnet, Canisbay or Bower, do not waste your time looking for some – at present it appears that there are no stone circles in that vicinity (Myatt 2003, 27). The difficulty in giving a precise number stems from the fact that many sites have clearly suffered more than their fair share of depredation and numerous stones – and entire stone circles – have been removed for reuse in more recent buildings.

> we read of the ransacking of the circles and of the ground closely surrounding those monoliths in search for treasure, gold and other precious objects. In our later days the spirit of utilitarianism prevailed, … greedy of every square foot of arable land, destroyed the weird and hoary monuments of our prehistoric county by breaking them up into fragments for our buildings or dykes or drains around our fields, or for metal on our roads (Gunn 1915, 21).

Whilst visiting Latheronwheel Bridge at the start of the last century, G. Gunn (1915, 8) recorded 'one of the finest specimens of stone circles in the north of Scotland'. However, on his return some years later he found that the site had been completely removed by the proprietor for cultivation purposes! Today, probably the best surviving stone circle

Fig 5.2 Guidebest stone circle

is at Guidebest, Latheronwheel Burn (Fig. 5.2). Approached from the modern road, the circle is set in a distinct hollow and moving downslope towards it there is an equally distinct sense of entering an amphitheatre, of which the circle creates a central focus. It is easy to imagine a community ranged along the slope watching or participating in a ceremony centred on or in the circle. There are also other remains in the area, standing stones and cairns, which may be contemporary with the circle. As built, the circle would have been about 190 feet in diameter, making it one of the biggest stone circles in the county (Burl 1995, 121). But today, only seven stones remain out of an original minimum of thirteen. This dilapidation is not unusual. Despite the few remaining stones at Latheron, Gunn (1915, 10) suggested that without doubt a stone circle had once stood there. Similarly, in the early twentieth century a stone circle was noted at Old Hall of Dunn, near Watten (RCAHMS 1911, 133, no. 483). Today, a solitary stone is all that remains. At Backlass some of the stones were stolen for a garden wall; a single standing stone may be the only remnant of what was once a large stone setting. What we see now of these monuments in no way reflects their original compositions.

Associated with the stone circles are a series of U-shaped stone settings that litter the county, the best example of which is that at Achavanich. It is possible of course that the U-shaped setting was originally a full oval, one end of which has since been destroyed. Today, 36 stones remain at Achavanich, but again, the original number may have been higher (RCAHMS 1911, 80); Gunn (1915, 10) suggested around fifty-four, whilst Thom, Thom & Burl (1990, 289) suggested around one hundred. The stones of this monument are set transversely to the circumference of the monument, unlike the majority of stone circles, in which they are set along the circumference. In addition, the stones appear to be set in a low bank or into the edge of a mound, which some suggest has resulted from a levelling of the site.

A similar history of stone loss is exhibited at the U-shaped setting at Broubster where the RCAHMS (1911, 44–46, no. 163) recorded only four fallen stones in 1911 whilst Thom, Thom & Burl (1990, 297) identified nine stones from a possible original total of 30 to 36. The progressive loss of stones from settings of all sorts is a theme not only noted in Caithness, but throughout Britain. In 1871, a plan made by Dryden of the stone rows at Hill o' Many Stanes showed that the monument comprised 250 stones, whereas Gunn had suggested that there were:

> originally 400 stones, but when I last visited them two years ago there were only 197, and of these some were broken away or lying on the ground. A large number have been removed for building or other purposes (Gunn 1915, 11).

Myatt's survey, in the 1980s, identified 180 visible stones (Myatt 1988, 282) but more recently, Dutton suggested that the monument comprised some 200 principal earth-fast stones and a further 540 small stones, set in 22 rows (Dutton 2003).

The many stone settings in and around Yarrows are also in various states of disrepair. Returning again to the settings at Garrywhin, we find that the number of actual stones differs from account to account. Dryden's plan (reproduced in Anderson 1886, 127) showed a total of 46 stones arranged in six rows. The RCAHMS (1911) survey indicates a total of 37 stones in eight rows. A more recent survey shows a total of 55 stones of which 47 are still standing (Freer & Myatt 1982, 61).

This variability in the definition of the monument itself will no doubt prove somewhat surprising to the visitor, but given the small size of the stones and the potential for vegetation like heather and bracken to obscure them, it is perhaps understandable. However, it does rather place a question mark over their proposed use as instruments or records of astronomical observation. To gauge the skies, it would surely be helpful to be able to see the instrument being used?

We have discussed the stone rows at some length, because of their unique connection with Caithness but in doing so, we are in danger of creating an unhelpful categorisation of what is, after all, a diverse set of monuments. Whilst we do not know the use either of U-shaped settings or of the stone rows and fan-shaped arrangements, it seems improbable that they had the same function. In both types, and indeed in the stone circles as well, we are dealing with vestigial monuments. It may ultimately prove to be our misfortune that their interpretation lies in the missing parts, not in the residue that survives to us; in this subsists their charm and their attraction. These are monuments for which one human being's opinion about their function is as valuable as any other's is: post-modern heaven. Go and look, and come up with your own interpretation.

As Macalister warned almost a hundred years ago, 'in considering Megalithic monuments of any kind, it must never be forgotten that what we see may be nothing but the skeleton of the original structure' (Macalister 1928, 304). However, the theft of stones is not without its consequences. And with regard to this we leave the final word to Lesley Myatt (1992, 45):

> It used to be a popular belief that gold would be found beneath the standing stones. That is one reason why a number of them have been removed or toppled. There were also superstitions attached to them. A farmer at Bruan is said to have removed one of the stones from Mid Clyth to use as a lintel over the fireplace of a kiln he was building. When the fire was lit the stone burst into flames but was not consumed in the process. So afraid was he that he returned the stone very quickly to the exact place in the row whence it had been removed.

The foregoing description of stone numbers for these monuments should not blind us to the fact that we do not know the date/s of their construction/s, their attribution to the Bronze Age being no more than wishful thinking. Neither do we know what they were used for. Alexander Thom seemed to argue that the stone fans were used to observe, measure and perhaps predict a very minor perturbation in the orbit of the moon, of around nine seconds of arc. In optimal conditions the human eye can resolve about two seconds of arc – a fact that may assist you in assessing the scale of the effect being observed. It would be difficult to achieve this level of observational precision if the starting point was an untidy line of very small stones laid out over a sloping hillside which may, as at Garrywhin, actually point downwards into the next hillside rather than outwards towards the distant horizon. These are not convincing observatories. They may have been used as calendrical devices that were potentially capable of exploring the relationship between lunar and solar cycles: the philosopher's stone for all prehistoric and early historic astronomy. Reconciling these cycles would allow the observer to create a calendar in which lunar months, a very useful time division, could be fitted into the solar year, the fundamental time division for all of nature: planting, harvesting, animal migrations, and so on. Furthermore, the pursuit of their reconciliation is not necessarily deterred by the fact that it is impossible over short intervals. In the fifth century BC, the Greeks discovered the Metonic cycle (named after Meton of Alexandria); it is a period of 19 years, in which the multiples of 19 years and 235 lunar (or synodic) months almost coincide; they remain about two hours out of sync. Since calendars are now freely available, it is difficult to imagine the significance that the determination of time and date held for humanity in the past. It is interesting, for example, that the Metonic cycle was used by the Early Christian Church – and is still used now – to calculate the date of Easter, the principal date in the liturgical calendar.

However, significant though this is, the use of a large area of small stones to identify the Metonic cycle, observationally, is enormously redundant. One would have to know the cycle to build the monument, so why would you build the monument at all? Perhaps as a public demonstration of your ability to do so? But even then, wooden poles would have been more precise markers and the selection of sites that were more level and had clear views to distant horizons would have made it all much simpler. The astronomical hypotheses have quite a way to go in order to prove convincing. Prehistoric humanity had pressing reasons to be interested in astronomy for navigational, horological and calendrical purposes, and we do not suggest otherwise. However, what we do suggest is that in considering the claims made for these stone settings, and their ilk, the Scottish judgement of 'not proven' is the only tenable one, given the available evidence.

6. BROCHS

Brochs, found only in Scotland and particularly in Atlantic Scotland, have captured the imaginations of scholars for centuries and are amongst the most studied monuments in British archaeology. The conventional view of a broch is that of a tall, imposing circular drystone tower, with cells or galleries contained within the thickness of the wall and which feature a range of complex architectural devices including: stairs; scarcements (to support wooden floors); lintel stones; stress-relieving gaps; and low single entrances with door rebates, bar-holes and guard cells (Fig 6.1; Fojut 1981; 150–151; Armit 2003, 55–78; Harding 2004, 109–123). Excavations have revealed traces of post-holes in the floors, which could have supported an internal wooden structure.

Fig 6.1 Schematic of a broch (copyright Alan Braby)

Right, here is the boring but necessary bit.

Although many scholars have called numerous roundhouses or grassy cairns/ mounds 'brochs' – no better shown than by some of the individuals who have worked in Caithness – recent studies have highlighted the complexity and variation of different building techniques and styles in the structural class. Once called brochs and duns, it is now commonplace to study these distinctive structures within the confines of Atlantic roundhouse terminology (see Armit 1992, 22–51; 1996, 109–36; 2003, 13–17 for overview). In brief: for some archaeologists, the term broch can be usefully applied only to those structures exhibiting key architectural features, most importantly a high hollow wall containing superimposed galleries. As Armit (2003, 16) reminds us, such a definition will obviously exclude any building that does not survive to height that is sufficient to display such features. It has become apparent to some scholars that the classic broch tower lies at one end of a 'spectrum of complexity' (*ibid.*), the other being represented by simple Atlantic roundhouses, as found at sites such as Bu (Hedges 1987), Pierowall (Sharples 1984), Quanterness (Renfrew 1979), Tofts Ness (Dockrill 2007) and St Boniface, Orkney (Lowe 1998). These low-walled structures are characterised by having no intramural features and stairs, and appear to have been built before brochs, around the first half of the first millennium BC.

Between broch towers and simple Atlantic roundhouses lie a wide range of roundhouse forms with varying degrees of architectural complexity. These complex Atlantic roundhouses include many of the structures that were often called brochs in past literature. In other words, the term Atlantic roundhouse describes all of the massive-walled drystone structures found in Atlantic Scotland, and contains a subset of more elaborate buildings known as complex roundhouses. Complex Atlantic roundhouses contain features such as intramural cells and stairs, but may not have been towers. Due to the vagaries of preservation it is impossible to know what proportion of complex roundhouses were originally broch towers (see Armit 2003, 16–17, Fig. 4 for an excellent summary). The progression from simple to complex may have taken place around 500 BC–200 BC. Often, enclosures were built around the roundhouses, as well as some outbuildings. These patterns culminated in the construction of the broch tower – a specialised form of complex Atlantic roundhouse – perhaps around 200 BC or thereabouts (see Armit 2003, 51). Good examples can be seen at Gurness and Howe, Orkney (Hedges 1987; Ballin Smith 1994). Around this time, nucleated villages – which surrounded the complex Atlantic roundhouses and broch towers – appeared in Orkney and Caithness (see Armit 1990, 438–40; Foster 1989). Although many of these sites continued to be used into later periods, the construction of complex Atlantic roundhouses appears to cease around AD 200. These developments were not paralleled everywhere. In the Western Isles, there are no nucleated settlements and isolated complex Atlantic roundhouses are the norm. This regional variation is shown by another distinctive structural type, the wheelhouse, which developed in the Western Isles but appears to be absent in Orkney and Caithness.

Hopefully, you are still with us. If you learn anything about brochs (or roundhouses!) it should be that Caithness has more examples per square kilometre than any other area of Scotland – there may be as many as 200. They are spread throughout the arable

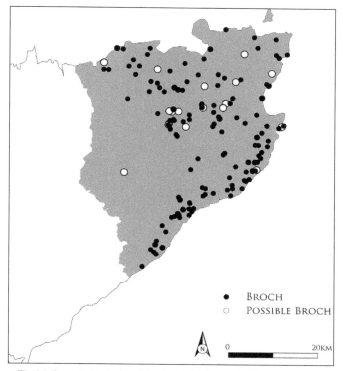

Fig 6.2 General distribution of brochs in Caithness after Swanson 1992, fig 6

land (Fig. 6.2; after Swanson 1992, 48–49, Fig. 6) and within these areas there are many roundhouse clusters hugging the coastline and meandering up river valleys. Caithness is the home of the broch. And they have, understandably, dominated many discussions.

By now we should be aware of another key fact: that the most important archaeological works of the county, be they excavations, surveys or overviews, were undertaken by individuals working during the nineteenth and early twentieth centuries. You will, therefore, be unsurprised to hear that our understandings of Caithness brochs are associated with a handful of individuals whose names should be familiar by now – Rhind, Anderson, Laing, Tress Barry and Nicolson.

Kettleburn

We have already admired Rhind for kick-starting interest in the county's archaeology, with particular regard to chambered cairns, but he was also integral to the birth and flowering of broch studies. In Scotland, one of the first brochs explored with the intention of obtaining and publishing useful information seems to have been the Howe of Hoxa on South Ronaldsay, Orkney, investigated by George Petrie in 1848. The clearing out of Backies broch near Golspie in Sutherland is equally memorable, as it was visited by J. J. Worsaae in 1848; he made some sketches, which are the only known

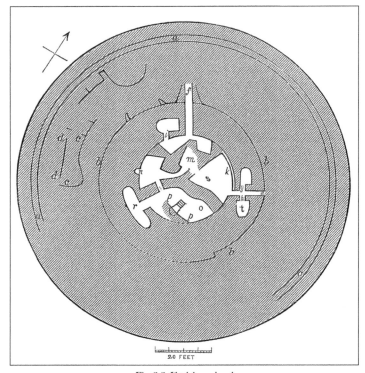

Fig 6.3 Kettleburn broch

surviving contemporary records (MacKie 2002, 31). It is against this sparse backdrop that we must view Rhind's inaugural excavations at Kettleburn broch (Fig. 6.3). His interest in brochs, which developed in a similar way to his rationale for excavating cairns, was spurred on by his ambition to analyse the structural details and contents of the homes of his ancestors.

As with his work on chambered cairns, he was meticulous in his attention to detail, which is shown no better than by his insistence on returning to Kettleburn broch after his excavation in order to supervise removal of his spoil heap during subsequent agricultural improvements (Rhind 1854a, 266). His work on brochs was multifaceted and groundbreaking. He had a great interest in analysing the evolution of the human race – to study the recovered artefacts so that he could '… form some idea of the progress in civilisation which the inhabitants of the Kettleburn House had attained' (Rhind 1853, 217). Chronology was equally important. In his lucid articles on his Kettleburn excavations he argued that some contemporaries 'ascribe to them [brochs] a more remote antiquity than existing data will warrant' (Rhind 1853, 221). It was largely because of the metal finds from his excavations and the absence of typical Neolithic objects that he argued that they should date to after the Neolithic period at the least. With his typical astuteness, he was one of the first scholars to note that broch sites were multi-phased and that the objects recovered related to different periods and peoples (*ibid.* 222).

Rhind was also passionate about the systematic recording and preservation of monuments and artefacts. One of the major, but underrated, legacies of Rhind's work was the gift of the Kettleburn objects to the National Museum of Antiquities. This formed the first collection made by the systematic excavation of a broch, and its components '... thus were possessed of inestimable value and interest' (Anderson 1883, 211). Anderson (*ibid.*, 211-212.) notes:

> In point of fact, the gift of this collection to the National Museum gave a new character to the collection of Scottish antiquities, and a new direction to the science of Scottish Archaeology. The Museum had previously been enriched by multitudes of donations of objects illustrating the unwritten history of the country, but they were mostly objects whose associations and relations were matters of inference and speculation. This group of objects, on the other hand, was one of which it could be said – (1) that they were related to each other by their common association with a single inhabited site; (2) that they all had relations with a certain typical form of sculpture; (3) that very various characteristics of form, material, art, and industry were shown to be thus inter-associated; (4) that the condition and culture of the occupants of the structure are truly disclosed by the study of this group of relics, in so far as the objects of which it is composed are capable of affording such indications; and (5) that the special knowledge thus acquired from one structure is also an important contribution to our general knowledge of the class to which it belongs.

YARROWS AND BROUNABEN

Despite excavating numerous Neolithic chambered cairns, Bronze Age cist burials, and possible Pictish burials during the 1860s Anderson also found time to excavate the broch complexes at Yarrows and Brounaben. Inevitably, the hand of Rhind continued to influence Anderson: his excavations were some of the first to be carried out under the auspices of the Rhind Committee of the Society of Antiquaries of Scotland.

A glance at the published plan of Yarrows shows that the site was multi-phased and comprised not only the broch but also a series of additional structures inside and outside the broch (Fig 6.4). Of the latter, there were two aisled buildings (C and D) which are now referred to as wags; structures G and F are more akin to Pictish cellular buildings. These buildings will be discussed later.

Discussion of both broch excavations was brief. For example, in his original 67-page 'Notice of the excavation of the brochs of Yarhouse, Brounaben, Bowermadden, Old Stirkoke and Dunbeath, in Caithness', read to the Society of Antiquaries of Scotland in 1871, only 15 pages are devoted to the publication of the structures and contents he uncovered during his two broch excavations. Indeed, his work at Brounaben just occupied one paragraph! This brevity was because Anderson was not excavating for excavation's sake. In keeping with his other excavations, Anderson wanted to use the structures, objects and human remains to formulate theories of wider relevance to British and European prehistory. The following decade Anderson published his second volume of *Scotland in Pagan Times*. In a chapter devoted to 'The Brochs and Their Contents'. Caithness comes into its own. Of the 50-page chapter, 40 per cent of the prose is taken up with discussion of the contents of five Caithness excavations: Kettleburn, Yarhouse, Old Strikoke, Bowermadden and Dunbeath. None of the broch sites excavated by Samuel Laing in and around Keiss merit a mention, but more of that later. He used the emerging data on brochs to move forward discussions about chronology and the emergence of civilisations and their relationship to one another. He was interested in all aspects of brochs: their origin (Celtic or Norwegian?); their multi-period nature and reuse of sites; what the artefacts told us about everyday life, trade and

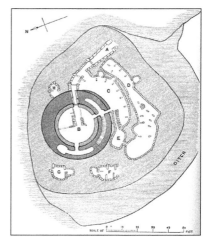

Fig 6.4 Yarrows broch

skill; the derivation of names such as 'burg' and/or broch. As well as publishing his own excavations, Anderson also found time to publish others. Prior to the 1870s the brochs at Ha' of Bowermadden, Achvarasdal Lodge, Dunbeath and Old Stirkoke were investigated by others to varying degrees. It fell to Anderson to publish the findings. He even used this opportunity to list and map as many Scottish brochs as he could find (Anderson 1890a). His excavations were a canvas onto which full and far-reaching discussions relating to the origin, chronology and history of a series of structures and artefacts could be painted. Anderson used excavations as a vehicle and stimulus for wider analyses of the role Scottish material played in the wider British and European context. The importance of Anderson to archaeology should be crystal clear by now – not only in terms of Caithness, but to the discipline in general. Anderson's scholarship was, at its best, challenging and provocative, rivalling that of the finest European scholars of his day (Clarke 2002, 1). His early endeavours put Caithness' archaeology at the forefront of British scholarship.

But, like Rhind and Shearer, Anderson's approach was that interpretations had to be founded on critical interrogation of the excavated evidence. Anderson had particular standards. He was adamant that archaeology should be based on the recording of facts, and that any interpretation should be built on scientific, inductive principles. Interpretation required accurate and exhaustive observation and to reach that level of expertise required ongoing training and experience (see Graham 1976, 286–7). This was outlined in various correspondence, lectures and publications in which Anderson stressed that the gathering up of local facts had to be done in a reliable, scientific manner – otherwise, any deductions drawn from them could not be depended upon:

For it is obvious that if the observations by which comparison and induction are accumulated have not been scientifically made, the conclusions drawn from them can have no scientific value, and that the first necessity in every scientific enquiry is accurate observation, exhaustive in its range, and recorded with the requisite precision and fullness of detail (Anderson 1881, 21).

Anderson, then, placed great importance on any investigation being as complete, exact and accurate as possible. As Clarke (2002, 8) reminds us, the espousing of such views was a reflection of the view that was current at the time, regarding science and its importance; but first and foremost it denotes the acceptance of the primacy of induction in the development of interpretations of the past. This is shown in Anderson's spat with James Fergusson between 1877 and 1878 concerning the origin of brochs. Anderson clearly followed an inductive mode, relying on a mass of factual data; Ferguson took a deductionist path and maintained that controversies of this sort tended to get 'smothered in detail'. He decided that once the main points are decided, the details will follow. Fergusson's paper was short on facts and relied mainly on abstract argument. Anderson's view was dismissed with the protest that one cannot allow the 'testimony of a few bits of bone or of rude pottery of very doubtful origin' to weigh against the general conclusions that were drawn from an abstract argument (see MacKie 2002, 33–4).

Anderson, then, strongly believed that close examination of the groups of artefacts recovered from brochs would allow us to arrive at conclusions as to the nature and quality of the culture and civilisation of their occupants (Anderson 1883, 234). This is almost identical to Rhind's view that analysis of the artefacts would enable us to '... form some idea of the progress in civilisation which the inhabitants of the Kettleburn House had attained' (Rhind 1853, 217).

Sir Francis Tress Barry and his Keiss estate

The excavation of any archaeological site, particularly brochs, is time-consuming and expensive. This situation was abundantly clear at the end of the nineteenth century. In his recommendations to the Society of Antiquaries of Scotland, Stuart (1868, 305) was at pains to stress that:

> The expense of clearing any of these ruins [brochs] would be very considerable, and it is doubtful if the work would be attended by any adequate result. ... There may be other cases where it would be prudent for the Society to *join in* such examinations, but I do not venture to recommend any general excavations in Pictish towers or "brochs", as the expense would very soon exhaust our fund.

How strange then that a few years later, Caithness was to witness the excavation of a dramatic number of brochs: between 1890 and 1910 more than one broch a year was excavated. Although the largest surviving broch in Caithness – at Ousdale (MacKay 1892) – was investigated during that period, any discussion about the investigation of brochs at that time should focus on the work of two figures: Sir Francis Tress Barry and John Nicolson.

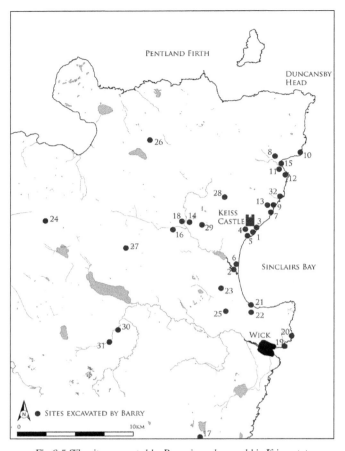

Fig 6.5 The sites excavated by Barry in and around his Keiss estate

Sir Francis Tress Barry's involvement in Caithness archaeology started in 1890, although his interest in the county no doubt started when he bought the Keiss estate (north-east Caithness) in 1881 (Baines 2002, 11); and it was this area that was the focus for his endeavours. Sir Francis Tress Barry had a distinguished career. He made his fortune in mining whilst working in Portugal. In 1846, he became vice consul for the Spanish province of Biscay, and a year later was appointed acting consul for the provinces of Biscay, Santander and Guipuzoca. From 1872, he was the consul general for the republic of Ecuador. Various honours were bestowed on him, including the Portuguese Order of Christ (1863), the Spanish Cross of Naval Merit (1880) and in 1876 he was created Baron de Barry of Portugal. In 1889, he was made a baronet by Queen Victoria and in 1890 he became the Member of Parliament for Windsor, a seat he held until 1906 (RCAHMS 1998, 5).

The 1911 RCAHMS Inventory asserts that Barry excavated 24 brochs (RCAHMS 1911, xxxi) whilst Anderson (1908) mentions 12. Irrespective of the total number, Barry excavated more brochs than any other individual (Fig. 6.5); and his endeavours were not restricted to roundhouses: he investigated other site types, including the chambered cairns at Earl's cairn, South Yarrows and Shean Stemster. He also returned to Moorland Mound where Laing had previously excavated (see Nicolson 1916, 314).

Between 1890 and 1895 Barry excavated at Keiss Harbour, Castle Lingas (or the large sandy mound at Birkle Hills, often known as Wester), Whitegate and Keiss Road. Between 1895 and 1897 he excavated Nybster, Everley and Skirza. The following year he excavated Freswick (Sands) and Ness. These sites were published by Anderson (1901) in his 'Notices of Nine Brochs along the Caithness Coast'. After a two-year break, during which he excavated a burnt mound, a fort, a midden and a chambered cairn, Barry returned to brochs and excavated the Hill of Works, Hillhead ('The Pap'), Elsay, Skitten (Kilminster), Green Hill (Reiss) and Acharole ('Baile a' Chairn') over a five-year period. Although all the sites were classed as brochs, recent programmes of survey and excavation suggest that there was great variety within the remains.

Although written accounts of Barry's investigations are incomplete, it is clear that his excavation techniques were coarse. He largely concentrated on the interiors of buildings and showed little concern for recording structural details or stratigraphic relationships. The proportions of the sites excavated also varied – some appear to have been completely cleared out (e.g. Keiss Harbour), others appear only to have been partially excavated.

Barry's work is traditionally viewed in a bad light. Referring to his work on chambered cairns, Davidson & Henshall (1991, 9) state, 'In the early years of this century three chambers in the north of the county were ineptly investigated by Sir Francis Tress Barry, an elderly English MP who had bought Keiss Castle'. The same dim view is taken of his broch excavations. In a paragraph entitled 'Continuing bad excavations' MacKie (2002, 34) states:

> A good example of the devastation caused by the crude standards of excavation of the turn of the century may be seen in the rapid exploration of some thirteen brochs in Caithness from 1894 onwards by Sir F. Tress Barry. Were it not for the fact that he was approached by Joseph Anderson who recorded and published as much of the resulting information as he could, probably nothing would have appeared in print at all. … They [the photographs] also show vividly the clutter of heaps of earth, workmen's shovels and barrows and half buried masonry which were typical of this rough and ready approach to archaeological digging at that time. When one considers these conditions it is a wonder that any useful information at all was recovered'.

These are harsh judgements. Barry did not pretend to be of the same ilk as Rhind and Anderson; he did not view himself as a competent archaeologist and, conscious of his weakness, he regularly sought advice from Rev. J. M. Joass and from Joseph Anderson. He was happy to entrust interpretation and analysis to more highly qualified individuals (see RCAHMS 1998, 6; Baines 2002, 13). And, whilst not excusing his techniques, we must remember that other contemporaries were equally exuberant in excavating numerous sites, Erskine Beveridge's work on North Uist being a good example (Beveridge 1911). As Batey (1984, 2) tells us, the fact that no other brochs have been located within the county's north-east coastal margin since Barry's work suggests that he had some form of organised approach to the identification of the sites that interested him.

Fig 6.6 Barry standing in Keiss Road (copyright RCAHMS)

Fig 6.7 Nicolson watercolour of Ballacharn broch (copyright RCAHMS)

Few written records survive of his work, and whilst they may have been destroyed, or lost, it is possible that Barry was simply not interested in written records. Instead, he gave greater precedence to other forms of recording. He was one of the first individuals to use photography extensively on archaeological sites in Scotland (Fig. 6.6). Barry clearly saw the value of photography and plans, and stated in his 1899 lecture to the Society of Antiquaries of London that:

> I took photographs of the more important points of interest. …These will also serve the purpose of giving a better idea of the appearance and structure of these Brochs conjointly with the plans than any mere written description can possibly do.

Sketches and watercolours were also crucial to his recording (Fig. 6.7). As well as being a crucial resource they also link us back to the important figure of John Nicolson who was central to many of Barry's investigations.

Barry never published any of his own work and the little insight we get into his ideals comes from a series of letters between himself and various correspondents, particularly Anderson, and three lecture manuscripts he presented. From these, we can discern some of his motivations, interests and interpretations.

The correspondence is particularly illuminating. We know that Barry frequently contacted Joseph Anderson and Rev Joass for advice (see Anderson 1901, 112). Anderson was out of the county for just over two decades before Barry commenced his work. Correspondence in the RCAHMS reveals an association with Anderson going back to 1890, and it is clear that Barry relied on Anderson, amongst others, as an archaeological mentor.

The three manuscripts – 'The prehistoric brochs of Caithness', 'Hillhead' and 'Suggested points to be considered in estimating the age of the Caithness brochs' – are equally illuminating.

In 1899, Barry read a paper entitled 'The prehistoric brochs of Caithness' (although it was only about his excavations at Keiss Harbour) to the Society of Antiquaries of London. In the opening paragraphs, he outlines his own views on his academic position:

> it would be the height of assumption on my part to attempt to address the Fellows of our Society posing as a scientific man, or one in any way specially qualified to draw conclusions from the interesting facts that I shall have the honour of bringing to your notice this evening. I make no such profession, but having been all my life more or less connected with mining operations, I naturally take great interest in delving into the crust of this material world, and endeavouring to ascertain what the result of such a search may be. I merely claim to have opened out these prehistoric ruins in a business and workmanlike manner.

Unlike Rhind, Anderson and others, it appears that Barry did not uncover archaeological information primarily to provide a basis on which he could further interpret and understand Caithness's prehistory. Barry's motivations appear to be more of intrigue – delving into the crust of the world in a workmanlike manner. Given his mining profession, it seemed natural for him to delve into seams, to find strata and follow them. He talks of his 'curiosity being excited' when told that Laing had discovered that Keiss Harbour was a habitation site and that there were still ruins to be uncovered.

Barry appears to have been more interested in uncovering, and possibly presenting, the sites than the actual post-excavation interpretation of the structural, artefactual and ecofactual remains that were discovered. Barry clearly did not remove all of the sites. It would have made little sense for him to do so. Indeed his passion for leaving visible entities in the ground after his work is dramatically shown by his memorial monuments: best demonstrated at Mervyn's Tower, Nybster (Fig. 2.3). This monument was built over Iron Age structures that Barry had uncovered; he included on it his name and the excavation date, by way of commemorating his work, and embellished it with decorative beasts and flags. Barry clearly felt that recording his own presence in stone in the landscape was as important as the archaeological remains he uncovered. However, he appears not to be the only person in Caithness concerned with exposing structures for 'public presentation' or curiosity. It is probable that W. S. T. Sinclair's 1866 investigations of Dunbeath broch were concerned more with exposing the broch structure than with the archaeological remains contained within the walls. Indeed, after the excavations the site was subsequently surrounded by a wall and trees were planted within the cleared interior. Also, the broch at Brounaban – excavated by Anderson and Shearer – may also have been restored after the excavation; the upper parts of the low inner wall face that survives are relatively loosely built to a standard height of about 1.5 metres (5 feet). The interior was also once used as a garden (RCAHMS 1911, 152, no. 511).

That said, it would be misleading to suggest that Barry did not use the uncovered remains as a prompt to ask wider questions related to prehistory. In particular, he had a clear interest in the age of the brochs. In his 1899 lecture, he commented that the multi-period nature of the site made it difficult to guess at the age of the brochs. He considers the age of the brochs more fully in his manuscript entitled 'Suggested points to be considered in estimating the age of the Caithness brochs'. He begins by asking 'Are they of the Stone, Bronze or Iron Age?' In his paper he identifies some of the bodies of evidence that may have helped to elucidate this question. He restates many previous arguments, particularly those espoused by Samuel Laing, who he seems to agree with. Like Laing before him (see below) he re-emphasises the fact that few bronze objects were found during his excavations. He also reiterates the fact that short cists were discovered over the broch at Oxtrow, Orkney and considers whether they could be Bronze Age. He refers to the find spot of the Roman pottery from Keiss Harbour, which was found at the top of the ruin, above at least six or seven floors of distinct separate occupations. This mirrors his comments in 1899:

On the very top of the debris stood part of a rough lunar-shaped wall, exhibiting signs of having been used in connection with living habitations. From its position it must have been the latest construction erected within the Broch. It was in a cavity at the bottom of this wall that the two pieces of Roman Samian ware, now exhibited, were found, and the iron implement was close by.

In his 1899 lecture, he notes that 'the articles became rougher and of a less civilised type, and at the bottom of the Broch (which had not been disturbed) the relics were of the roughest description, more particularly the pottery, of which there was little'. He ends his 'Suggested points to be considered in estimating the age of the Caithness brochs' paper by pondering: 'Is it not possible that these Brochs belong to the Neolithic or Early Bronze Age?'

Such a viewpoint sets Barry at loggerheads with Anderson. Indeed, it aligns Barry more with one of Anderson's contemporaries, Samuel Laing. As we shall see later, Laing's views did not meet with widespread, if any, acceptance and it is fair to surmise that Barry's suggestions would have been dismissed in the same way. Although we do not know when Barry wrote his 'Suggested points to be considered in estimating the age of the Caithness brochs', notes within the document suggest that it was after Anderson's 1883 and 1886 *Scotland in Pagan Times* volumes. This makes Barry's views on the date of brochs even more puzzling. Barry was in direct contact with Anderson and must have been acutely aware of Anderson's views, including his opinion on the date of brochs. Given this, it seems odd that it was Anderson who published the only record of Barry's work (Anderson 1901).

Graham (1976, 290) believes that Anderson wrote his 1901 paper to 'save something from the wreck of improperly recorded excavations'. Given the contrasting views of Anderson and Barry and their perception in the twentieth and twenty-first centuries, one has to ask why Anderson felt the need to be at all involved in Barry's 'devastation', 'bad excavations' and 'rough and ready' work (MacKie 2002, 34).

To answer the question we need to return once more to the rationale and ideals of Anderson, again through reference to his published works. This is not always straightforward – although Anderson clearly had personal views on, for example, the study and collection of artefacts, he did not often feel the need to make them explicit (Clarke 2002, 5). One certainly searches in vain for reasoning in his report on Barry's investigations (Anderson 1901). The need to report on Barry's work was probably the result of what Anderson saw as the key components of his worldview: the gathering of data from as wide a field as possible by using scientific and recorded methods (Clarke 2002, 7).

> Every recorded fact is an addition to the sum total of our general knowledge of the subject; and though in isolated circumstances it may seem of little importance, yet when marshalled in its proper place among the rest of the facts accumulated, it may prove to be the missing link which makes the demonstration complete. It is this gathering up of the local facts, and storing them for future use in your Proceedings, which constitutes the value of such a society as yours, and becomes an aid to the systematic study of Scottish archaeology (Anderson 1890b, 353–4).

Given that Anderson felt these ideals should permeate Scottish archaeology (Clarke 2002, 7) this surely suggests that he felt that he approved of the manner in which Barry was undertaking his endeavours. This is certainly indicated at the beginning of Anderson's 1901 paper where he notes that prior to Barry's work only five brochs had been excavated 'completely and systematically for the purpose of scientific record' (*ibid.* 113): Kettleburn, Yarrows, Brounaben, Dunbeath and Ousdale. He dismisses Laing's work as partial digging. In the stroke of a sentence, Anderson groups Barry alongside himself and Rhind. Although clearly influenced by the large number of structures that Barry investigated, Anderson (*ibid.*) nonetheless records that, 'Sir Francis Tress Barry has done more to elucidate the structure and contents of the brochs than has ever been done in Caithness before by all the investigators together'.

He concludes (*ibid.* 145) that:

> The evidence derived from a comparison of the results of Sir Francis Tress Barry's excavations with those of previous investigations goes rather to confirm than to extend in any great measure our knowledge of the structure and contents of the brochs. Yet in certain directions new items have been added to the sum of that knowledge.

And in this paragraph we may have the clues. These 'items' that have added to the sum of our knowledge include new finds of animal remains; recovery of objects never seen before, such as painted pebbles; and new features of broch situation, construction and association. Although there is no equivalent to the discussion seen in his previous broch publications Anderson ends the article with a return to issues concerning the age and origins of the brochs. In true Anderson fashion he does not put forward 'conjectural theories' but restricts himself to theories arrived at through the scientific evidence afforded by the excavated data (the structures and their contents). In apparent reference to earlier scholars' statements, Anderson stresses that rudeness in aspects of construction is no criterion for remote antiquity and the types of implements that are truly characteristic of the Stone and Bronze Ages do not occur amongst the broch relics. He concludes again that the broch structure may have had its origin in the civilisation of the Late Celtic period (*ibid.* 148).

Anderson probably accepted that Barry's techniques were coarse – though perhaps no coarser than his own – but he would gladly describe, accept, record and ultimately display the finds Barry uncovered. Indeed, Anderson believed that landowners who failed to donate objects found on their estates ran the risk of being branded unscientific (Clarke 2002, 8). Anderson would have preferred that objects were at least published, admittedly in a limited way, rather than simply stored away. As Clarke (2002, 9) highlights, it is of little surprise that during Anderson's keepership the collections of the National Museum of Antiquities grew enormously. Anderson strongly believed in the accumulation of records: for him, the records were objects.

THE KEISS CLUSTER

In the middle of Barry's nineteenth-century estate is the wonderful village of Keiss, set in a low rolling landscape now given over to mixed arable cultivation and pasture. As we have seen, the area is rich in archaeological and historical remains, ranging from Pictish burials through to twentieth-century concrete pillboxes. The area is also home to what could be the densest distribution of roundhouses in Scotland. There are three: Keiss Road, Keiss Harbour, and Whitegate, all situated within a 500-metre radius (Fig. 6.8). Samuel Laing appears to have excavated at Keiss Harbour and Keiss Road during the 1860s, and four decades later Barry and Nicolson undertook further excavations and also began work at Whitegate.

After their excavations, Laing and Barry donated many artefacts to the National Museum of Antiquities. This dataset was a welcome addition to the nation's collection

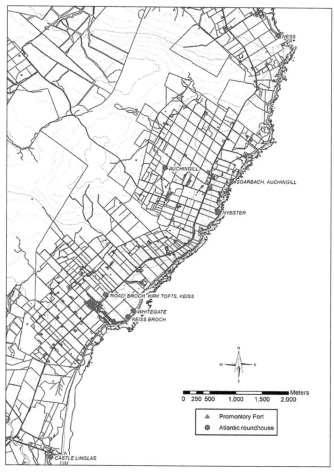

Fig 6.8 Location of the brochs at Keiss Road, Keiss Harbour, and Whitegate. This is one of the densest roundhouse distributions in mainland Scotland.

and aided Anderson's assertion that we will only ever understand our archaeology by the systematic collection and study of all existing materials illustrative of her native industry and native art, along with their associated indications of social organisation and potential culture. So what do the finds and the analysis of their context tell us?

Various authors, including ourselves, have highlighted how Keiss appears to have been an important focus of activity from around the middle of the first millennium BC to the late first millennium AD. Although the early publications give no indication of any phasing, a resurvey has indicated that the roundhouses and associated external complexes were multi-phased and occupied over a long period of time, although we cannot tell whether occupation was continuous. This longevity is supported by the finds. For example, the pottery and Roman finds clearly indicate occupation in the first three centuries AD (Fig. 1.11), whilst the nail-headed pin (and perhaps the 'Pictish' painted pebble) suggest later activity, probably during the Pictish period.

Re-walking the land has also illustrated that the Keiss roundhouses were larger functioning units than indicated by traditional understanding. They were not isolated buildings: they all contain a consistent set of further components including external structures (Fig. 6.9). Indeed, the latter are as common in Caithness as they are in Orkney. It is, therefore, possible that within the maze of hollows and unexcavated areas there are nuclear settlements similar to examples elsewhere, such as the aforementioned Gurness complex in Orkney.

At a broad inter-site level, analysis of the artefacts demonstrates that the inhabitants of Keiss engaged in long-distance trade, crafts, and consumption of high-status goods and materials. The fragments of decorated Samian ware, fine ware and the glass vessel illustrate that Roman material was reaching the area between the first and third/fourth centuries AD. X-ray fluorescence analysis reveals that the crucible from Keiss Harbour was used for melting tin bronze with notable inclusions of lead and zinc. The zinc indicates access to a metal pool that was ultimately of Roman origin; such reuse and recycling activity is recognised on other native (i.e. non-Roman) sites and monuments. The range of goods shows that the inhabitants of Keiss were part of a limited group of northern sites with access to Roman material and the area is clearly of significance within the region.

This pattern is supported by other finds. In recent studies, aspects of craft production have been interpreted as high status, for example ferrous and non-ferrous metalworking. Similarly, the rough-out for the triangular weaving tablet from Keiss Harbour may suggest restricted access to wider aspects of textile working. These plaques were used for the manufacture of elaborate borders on woven textiles. When taken individually the status of these finds could be queried, but cumulatively they point to sites of some status.

The final point of interest is, of course, the proximity of the three sites to one another. In other areas such as Shetland and the Western Isles, brochs are regularly spaced one kilometre or more apart. In neighbouring Orkney, several dominate 3.5 kilometres of coastline. Caithness roundhouses are more clustered, particularly the three Keiss examples. This broch density is even more marked when we consider that on the same bay, to the north and to the south, lie Nybster and Wester roundhouses. Intriguingly, this coastal clustering is repeated 6 kilometres to the north at Freswick Bay

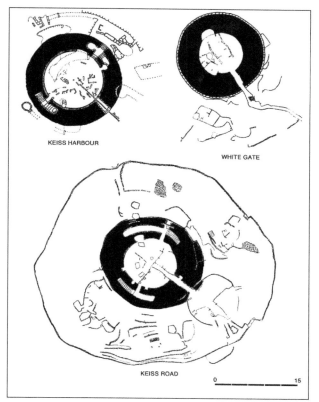

Fig 6.9 The Keiss roundhouses; note the differences in size and structural composition and the hints at outbuildings

with Skirza, Ness, and Freswick roundhouses situated on the shore, the first two on cliff tops, and Everley 500 metres inland, all four occurring within a radius of less than one kilometre (Fig. 6.10).

In many archaeological circles one often hears individuals talking about 'their relationship with the heritage' and/or desire to use archaeology to 'give something back to the local community'. Few people deliver on the offer but certain people do. This certainly applies to the small staff (Rhona MacPherson, Maureen Miller and the other staff members) at Keiss Primary School who should be held in the highest regard for the outstanding commitment and ingenuity they have shown in bringing archaeology to the pupils, thus enabling them to have a better knowledge of, and affinity with, their archaeology, particularly brochs.

Nybster

The formulation of close and enduring relationships between local communities and their archaeological heritage is, of course, not a new concept. It has always run through

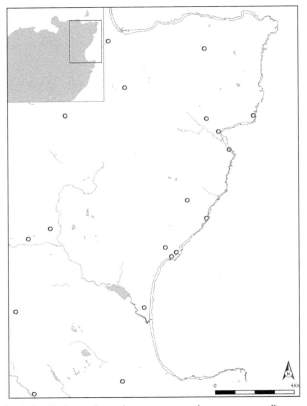

Fig 6.10 Broch distribution up the north-east coast; note the numerous roundhouses scattered up and down the coast

the veins of Caithnessians, but particularly so in the case of the individuals that live around Sinclair's Bay and Freswick Bay. We have seen that in many antiquarian endeavours local people have been central to the outcomes. This has involved taking part in excavation, granting permission for people to work on their land, recording and disseminating information, and even constructing commemorative monuments. Indeed, were it not for the local people, much information would have been lost to future generations.

For us, the relationship between Tress Barry and John Nicolson stands out as an exemplar. An extract from a letter written to Nicolson by Barry in 1906, five months before the latter died, illustrates the backgrounds and working relationship of the two:

My dear Nicolson, I am sending you two parcels by Post. One contains two plans of Caithness, the other a letter from me as to what I want you to do to them. ... Possibly my Butler, Webb, may have seen you and told you that I was writing about all this.

The fact that Nicolson worked with Barry for a number of years demonstrates that whatever their social differences they relied on each other during and after the excavations. Not only did Nicolson appear to take responsibility for much of the excavation he also recorded the structures and artefacts. Nicolson also took great pride in the monuments and discoveries after the excavation seasons were long over. From his home he could see one of the most important archaeological complexes in northern mainland Scotland, at Nybster (Fig. 6.11). Nybster is home to a myriad of later prehistoric structural remains including a promontory fort and a roundhouse, as well as other outbuildings that are scattered across the peninsula. As well as excavating on the site, photographs and anecdotal information suggests that Nicolson maintained the site in the years after excavation. For whatever reason, he had a strong desire to maintain and remember the archaeology, the work and the people. And for him, the visible remains were central.

At numerous points throughout this book we have touched on the lack of visibility of much of Caithness' remains owing to the lack of care for the few sites that have been revealed. This, unfortunately, is now the case at Nybster. Despite the sterling efforts of Nicolson's grandson, Alistair Sutherland, there is no state or government maintenance of the site. This is a great pity as Nybster, in our opinion, is the jewel in the broch crown of northern mainland Scotland. The lack of care and maintenance of the present day site severely hinders any chance of enjoying – let alone understanding – the range, style and quality of the archaeological remains uncovered by Barry and Nicolson.

But, before we all rush out to petition groups and individuals to take urgent action, we need to return again to our earlier discussion of appropriate avenues of conservation, interpretation and public presentation. We have seen in our analysis of chambered cairns that it is difficult to find a balance between making a site readily understandable and presentable, and portraying the complexities of the site's life histories and the

Fig 6.11 Aerial view of the impressive Iron Age complex at Nybster (courtesy of www.sinclairaerialsurveys.com)

different personalities who excavated the remains. Even if we label one of Barry's sites a 'broch' it is entirely misleading to suggest that what is seen on the ground today is an accurate reflection of the original monument. It is an imprint of the nineteenth-century archaeologists' work. We have seen that much of the Caithness footprint was cast in the nineteenth century and, furthermore, that during that time different people used different excavation strategies and techniques, all of which greatly influenced what proportion of the structure saw the light of day. Not all sites were fully excavated, but others were largely removed. Some investigators were unconcerned about what would happen to the site after excavation – a consideration that we would now call 'long-term management and preservation' – whereas others actively reconstructed parts of the monuments. Some individuals took no interest in what the monument would look like after excavation, or what a visitor would see. Understanding the present day appearance of Caithness sites is, therefore, a complex undertaking. This is particularly true of the grassy mounds excavated by Barry and Nicolson. Their approaches to excavation had a marked effect on the preservation and future experiences of the sites.

However, these idiosyncrasies are exactly what make the sites even more exceptional. As well as being exceptional Iron Age complexes, they are markers of the investigative process and the imprints of the individuals who uncovered the brochs. These should be embraced in any dialogue about, and engagement with, the site. But this, again, goes against the normative presentations of brochs across Scotland – many, if not all, presentations depersonalise the investigative process, to the extent that the individuals who excavated the sites are excluded from the majority of presentational narratives. This is particularly acute when dealing with sites investigated in the Victorian period. Yet these individuals to greater or lesser degree manufactured the sites we now see. How can they not be part of the story?

Let us for a moment step out of Caithness into the neighbouring county of Sutherland and consider the broch site at Carn Liath. The 3rd Duke of Sutherland first investigated the site in 1868 (Joass 1890). The following century was not kind to the site and dilapidation caused by natural means and petty vandalism, coupled with the unsanctioned building up of spurious 'secondary' features, altered the broch's appearance and threatened its fabric to such an extent that emergency consolidation was proposed in 1967. The suggested works included the infilling of the guard cell and stairs, and the raising of the floor level to protect internal features. Unauthorised clearance of the broch's interior by a school party in 1971 aroused fears that any surviving archaeological levels might have been penetrated. Furthermore, the masonry extracted had acted as a stabilising agent and its removal created a potentially dangerous situation. In response to this threat, the broch's interior was given an archaeological clean-up in 1972 by our old friend J. W. Corcoran who, we remember, was also undertaking similar work at Camster chambered cairn. After his work, the site was taken into state care (see Love 1989, 157 for overview) and you can still visit it today.

Paula Love undertook another programme of work in 1984 and 1986–7. The work had two main aims: to ascertain the degree (if any) of stratigraphical preservation on site; and 'to improve the appearance of visible features as an aid to visitor appreciation of the monument' (Love 1989, 157). To enhance visitor appreciation of the site, some of the broch's structural and internal features were reinvestigated (Love 1989, 159). Some features were reopened, such as the backfilled guard cell, whilst others were filled in for safety. External features were also investigated again with the dual aim of increasing archaeological knowledge and exposing the surviving remains as part of an ongoing programme of consolidation for public display (Love 1989, 160).

The 1980s team clearly appreciated the issues faced in re-excavating sites that had initally been excavated by antiquarians. First, an appreciation of the degree of physical disturbance caused by Victorian excavations. Second, the need for meticulous recording of any masonry removed, in anticipation of its subsequent reinstatement, and adherence to the caveat that excavation should not significantly outpace consolidation. Third, the understanding that the requirements of research must be sensitively balanced against the needs for preservation (Love 1989, 157). Love also notes that re-examination of areas first investigated by others is problematic:

> the degree of disturbance left as a legacy of the Victorian excavations was only discernible after considerable and, in retrospect, seemingly wasted efforts on the part of the team, where superficially fruitful areas of investigation had been rendered totally devoid of stratigraphy by the 19th-century excavators (Love 1989, 157).

Referring to the north-east outbuilding she states (*ibid.* 165):

> It soon became clear however that the Third Duke had hacked indiscriminately through all the archaeological levels, down to natural soil, leaving isolated masonry features which could not be tied into any logical chronological sequence. These included: (1) a raised paved feature with uprights, similar to those mentioned by Joass (Joass 1890, 104), in the SE corner of the outbuilding; (2) a stretch of raised, coursed walling abutting (1) above; (3) a stretch of raised, coursed masonry lying next to the broch, again in the SE corner; and finally (4) a stretch of curved walling adjacent to the broch wall in the SW corner of the outbuilding.

However, her attitude to the preservation of these rediscovered features appears ambivalent:

> These features were excavated, recorded and removed, but their reinstatement in any future consolidation of the outbuilding seems unlikely, divorced as they were from any secure stratigraphical context. Their function remains similarly conjectural in the absence of any diagnostic finds. … Excavation was perforce piecemeal, not to mention frustrating for those involved (Love 1989, 165).

Love seems to imply that structural elements with relationships to the broch and its sediments that are poorly understood, or not understood at all, cannot, or should not, be reinstated. We strongly disagree.

If anyone was ever brave enough to tackle the presentation of the brochs in and around Sinclair's Bay then we would, again, espouse an approach that focusses as much on the imprints of the personalities who excavated the sites as the archaeology. Earlier, we called this an'investigation biography'. 'Biography' means, of course, the 'written record of the lives of individual men as a branch of literature' (OED). We employ the term investigation biography to denote two separate but closely related things: the investigation of a particular archaeological investigator's life and work, and the impact of the motivations and methodologies of that individual on the survival of particular remains at a given monument. This is certainly not a new concept. Marshal McLuhan (1967) famously asserted that 'environments are not passive wrappers' and both the physical environment that survives the archaeological excavation of a monument and the reportage of the exercise modify every subsequent perception of that monument. Some archaeologists are conscious of these factors, but in Caithness it is even more important than usual to take cognisance of the distorting lenses of antiquarian manipulation of sites, particularly brochs. Certainly, any interpretation for these sites must consider the extent to which they, or aspects of them, are artefacts of their discovery and revelation. The work of Brian Smith in Shetland, in particular on the Broch of Clickhimin, indicates that this process is not unique to Caithness.

We have noted how Barry's life and background undoubtedly affected his techniques and attitudes to excavation. His mining background was clearly influential. His professional experience of following geological seams makes it of little surprise that he drove cuttings into broch mounds and followed structural 'seams' until they crossed with others. He clearly had experience at supervising the removal and management of large masses of material. Photographs and surviving stone mounds illustrate that he was meticulous in his control of soil and stone spoil. Health and safety considerations of a sort characterise his work: wheelbarrow runs were put in place to ensure safe passage and 'danger' signs were erected (Fig. 6.12).

These factors greatly influenced the sites we visit today, and a visit to any of Barry's sites is a confusing one. Let us return once again to Nybster. Here, some features are interpretable – the roundhouse is clear enough – whilst other structures are confusing masses of undistinguished walls, and their relationship to one another is entirely perplexing. Many 'walls' are not walls, merely artefacts of Barry's wall-chasing trenches. Some are the rear elevations of stone faces from which the wall matrix has been excavated away. Further, there are many large stone settings the interpretation of which, in terms of the structural architecture of the site, is anomalous to say the least. For example, at Nybster there are numerous flat stones set horizontally across negative features. These are not crucial elements of some Iron Age subterranean structure but temporary works for wheelbarrow runs used by Barry's workmen. At the same site there are three conspicuous mounds: two are Barry's spoil heaps, another is the original core for Mervyn's Tower, the bombastic monument that is as imposing as the excavated archaeology.

Mervyn's Tower is the most impressive but others exist: for example, at Ness. The sculptures are of a type we may describe as 'vernacular' and are not without cultural value in their own right. Crucial components of the monuments were plaques stating

Fig 6.12 Photograph of work at Hillhead, showing the numerous barrow runs and health and safety signs (copyright RCAHMS)

Barry's name and the date of excavations, as well as carvings of beasts, grotesques and even flags. Yet they were sometimes more than simple commemorative pieces. The monument at Nybster provided a raised walkway from which the confusion of structures on the site could be viewed. It was also a prominent landmark, viewed from the sea and the desire to retain this 'beacon' as a navigational aid no doubt influenced the selection of the site to which it was subsequently relocated. The connection between the Nybster monument and local shipping is emphasised by the existence of other cognate 'monuments' at the Nybster pier and slipway. One of these acts as a signpost to Nybster broch and to a promontory fort at Sgarbach. Importantly, some of these monuments were built over Iron Age structures (uncovered, then backfilled). Barry clearly felt that recording his own presence in stone in the landscape was as important as the archaeological remains he uncovered. To add to the confusion, the present location of Mervyn's Tower at Nybster is, as we have noted, not where it was first erected. In the 1980s, the shell of the monument was moved in front (landward side) of the broch, but the core was left.

Barry probably saw himself as a collector in the great Victorian tradition: in his case, of sites (see Baines 2002, 13). He was keen on having impressive monuments on his estate. The presentation of the site during and after excavation was as important as the process of discovering the archaeology. He clearly did not remove the entire site; within his rationale, it would have made little sense. However, Barry's emphasis was on the – often spectacular – monumental remains that his work exposed, even at the cost of slighting the sediments and artefact assemblages associated with those monuments (he incorporated a number of quern stones into his memorial structures). Barry's emphasis on the presentation of the monuments is exemplified by the tantalising suggestions of rebuilding and maintenance on his sites, which was undertaken either during or after his excavations. Comparison of Barry's photographs with recent resurveys of some of the sites carried out by the authors has recognised differences in the appearance of stonework and masonry; this suggests that, in the post-investigation period, individuals felt it necessary to maintain and rebuild parts of the monument in order to maintain the buildings' fabric and integrity – and memories of the past.

All of these wonderful idiosyncrasies should be enjoyed and interpreted, not airbrushed from the record. We need an approach that gives the individuals and communities who investigated and cared for the archaeology a central role: if we do not, we will be treating our archaeological monuments as neutral, depersonalised spaces which have little or no connection to people and communities. Indeed, there is much to be gained from presenting sites in their community context – this allows them to be actively and continuously interpreted and reinterpreted *in situ*. And in this process, contemporary local personalities who have a passion for the monuments must be treated as equal partners.

The Keiss Primary School's children and its teachers, such as Rhona and Maureen, demonstrate that there is still a strong relationship between local communities and their archaeological heritage. No story of the area is complete without reference to John Nicolson's formidable grandson, Alistair Sutherland. Alistair lives in the very house occupied by Nicolson during Barry's investigations. Over many years Alistair has attempted to maintain the bond between the Auckengill community and the roundhouses through creating and running the John Nicolson Museum, which is sited directly across the road from his house and is now the home of the Caithness Broch Centre. Alistair is, without question, one of the most passionate and formidable people we have ever met – not just in the county, but in the country. But he is also the epitome of a gentle giant. His enthusiasm and passion is inspiring. He continues to take great pride in the archaeological remains at Nybster and beyond. This was shown clearly in the summer of 2004 when, over a hundred years after his grandfather's original work, he helped us strim the overgrown, offensive grass at Nybster and Keiss Road to facilitate resurvey of the sites. He is one of the most inspiring people we have met on our journey and is one of the reasons – or perhaps the sole reason – why we continue to work in the area. We only wish we could do more. One of us (AH) established the Caithness Broch Centre with the aim of creating a tribute to Alistair, his family and the community. For Alistair's unremitting patience, we offer our heartfelt thanks – and for our failings, we offer our sincere apologies.

7. WAKING THE DEAD: IRON AGE BODY PARTS

CROSSKIRK

Over 1,600 years ago on the north coast of mainland Scotland, a middle-aged or elderly man was living out his final days. Once well built and muscular, he was now riddled with osteoarthritis that seriously disabled him and made it difficult for him to eat. He lived and worked in and around Crosskirk broch, an important site from the first millennium BC to the first millennium AD, which was prominently situated on the northern cliffs. He spent many days looking across the water to Orkney, particularly fascinated with the upstanding and outstanding geological formation now known as the Old Man of Hoy. He had visited it many times.

It was winter when he passed away. His friends and relatives chose to bury him at the heart of their community. They chose to bury him in an enclosure outside the broch. He was buried in a cist in the floor immediately beside the heart of everyday life – the hearth. But Crosskirk man was not buried lying down, covered, and hidden from view. He was seated upright facing the Old Man of Hoy. (Fig. 7.1).

In today's westernised world the term 'burial' is usually synonymous with the act of disposing of corpses, usually as inhumations, in concealed areas that are well beyond the immediate domestic sphere. This has, in turn, led many archaeologist to be concerned with similar formal practices, hence the study of various forms of cist burials, be they Pictish, Christian or Viking, in isolated parts of the landscape. This has led not only to the assumption that in the case of most burials the remains were placed in some form of conventional concealed container, but also that burial practices and rituals were separate from the domestic arena. Crosskirk man clearly shows that at certain periods this was not the case and we must, therefore, be cautious in making distinctions between ritual, death and domesticity. Indeed, recent studies (e.g. Bradley 2005) have stressed that the supposed separate spheres of domestic life, death and ritual may have been closely linked, if not inseparable at certain junctures in prehistory. There were periods when death kicked down the doors of the domestic sphere.

Crosskirk man was buried in a time that has been conventionally labelled as the Iron Age – that is, the time between 800BC and AD800. We have already seen that in these two periods, burial took place in the way we find familiar today : individuals were

Fig 7.1 The burial at Crosskirk (copyright RCAHMS, Horace Fairhurst Collection)

buried in cists with some form of above-ground marker. But things appear to have been different in the Iron Age. Three recent works are important in assisting our attempts to understand how bodies were treated during this long period (Mulville *et al.* 2003; Armit & Ginn 2007; Tucker & Armit 2009). These studies demonstrate that despite the small – and undoubtedly skewed – data set, it is fairly clear that there were a multiplicity of burial rites, which involved a complex and evolving set of attitudes to the human body, its display, curation, and disposal. These practices involved various parts of the body: articulated skeletons, disarticulated skeletal remains, cremated human remains and worked human bone.

Other Caithness evidence

Human bodies and body parts are consistently, if in small numbers, found across Atlantic Scotland, particularly during excavations of brochs and/or Atlantic roundhouses. In other words, many excavations of domestic spheres have produced body parts. Armit & Ginn (2007, 116) highlight the strong regional focus in Orkney and Caithness. Of the 37 sites listed by them 11 (or 30 per cent) are from Caithness and all from sites which had, at some point, an Atlantic roundhouse as a focus.

Armit & Ginn (2007) rightly highlight the difficulties in assessing the finds from old excavations, and, rightly, discount antiquarian and vague references to the recovery of bodies. However, although we accept all of these points and freely admit that many may post date the Iron Age, it is pertinent to note that, to the authors' knowledge, over 30 Caithness broch sites have references to human remains being found on them. In other words, more than half of the investigated Caithness brochs have produced evidence for human remains. In keeping with the wider Atlantic pattern they fall into four main forms: articulated remains (of which some were in cists), disarticulated remains, cremation and worked human bone.

Naturally, not all of these need date to the Iron Age. Archaeological records and historical texts demonstrate that the broch mounds were used for burials long after they were first built and had gone out of use. In an archaeological sense, a particular focus has been the Viking period, which is represented well by the recovery of a pair of tenth-century oval tortoise brooches and other objects associated with a skeleton from Castletown broch in 1786 (Wilson 1863, 265–6; Anderson; 1874, 549–51). The location of the short cist at Westerseat that contained the tortoise brooches was 'on the top of a mound of gravel … a little below the Broch of Kettleburn' (Anderson 1874, 551), which suggests again that the broch mound was a factor in the place of burial. Indeed, when considering Viking burials on such sites, Anderson suggests that: 'This is what we should expect of a Norwegian burial of the period when a "how" or mound was always selected or made for the interment' (1874, 550; see also Anderson 1890a, 175–8). Historical and oral traditions also suggest that broch mounds were used for burials until recent times. Therefore, it may be pertinent to suppose that most of the formal cist burials from brochs are later in date. But Crosskirk man adds a note of caution to this assumption. Further, whereas in the past 'formal' inhumation burials in cists were generally assumed to be restricted to later periods, recent excavations have shown that the tradition may have its inception in the Iron Age. Given the Crosskirk evidence, it may be necessary to rethink the articulated cist burial at Brounaben broch, which was found by the side of the door to the broch. Need it post-date the broch, as was once believed by Anderson (1890a, 132)?

And what of the articulated remains that were not found in a formal cist? A human skeleton, head downwards, covered with small stones and a little earth was discovered in a narrow opening over the entrance to the stairs at Ousdale broch in 1891 (MacKay 1892, 354). Anderson (1890a, 185) records a human skeleton that was covered by a flagstone and laid close to the wall of the broch at Borrowston. Similarly, Tress Barry found two crushed human skeletons in a 'roof-less chamber', presumably an intramural feature, at Barroch broch; we need not agree with his suggestions that they were crushed and killed in their sleep (n.d., 9). Aside from the cist already mentioned at Brounaben broch, Anderson (1890a, 142) noted the remains of another human skeleton in the chamber at the foot of the stairs. There are, of course, problems with dating these events, but not all of them necessarily post-date the Iron Age.

We are on slightly surer chronological footing when considering the other group of data: disarticulation – particularly of the skull. Again, not all disarticulated remains need be Iron Age in date. For example, of the five separate deposits of human remains uncovered at Yarrows – some intermingled with ash and refuse – none convincingly dates to the Iron Age, or to the broch's construction (Anderson 1890a, 131–2). However, other broch excavations suggest that there may be a closer link between disarticulated remains and the Iron Age.

During excavations of a chamber at Kettleburn broch four pieces of human cranium were recovered in one of the intramural galleries; the pieces were embedded in a heap of ashes which also contained pottery and a bone weaving comb. Examination of some human remains by Quekett revealed the upper end of a tibia, a portion of the parietal bone of an adult's cranium and molar teeth from a young subject (Rhind 1853, 216, 223). This apparent use of the human body, often with a particular focus on skulls, may allow us to venture back into other nineteenth-century references. At the start of the last century, Sir Francis Tress Barry gave a lecture on his excavations of the Hillhead and Barroch (Hill of Works) brochs to the Society of Antiquaries of London. During a discussion of the articles found at Hillhead he noted that the top of a human skull with three holes bored in it, forming a triangle, was recovered from the floor of the entrance passage (see also RCAHMS 1911, xxxv, 162). The skull has recently been dated to AD310-440 (Tucker & Armit 2009, 215)

Although there is no record of exactly where they were found, Tress Barry also recovered human skull fragments from Whitegate, Wester and Nybster brochs. During excavations of the broch mound at Keiss Harbour Samuel Laing recovered the fragment of a human lower jaw, apparently of a six-year-old (Laing & Huxley 1866, 28–9, Figs 41 and 42). Laing notes that the human remains came from a secondary midden (*ibid.* 23–4, 28, Figs 34 and 36). Although we have no idea when the bone was deposited – although it must at least post-date the construction and initial use of the broch – it could be inferred again that parts of human skulls were deposited on broch sites during the Iron Age. If we add in the references to the 40 human skulls that were recovered during investigations at the Burn of Latheronwheel broch (RCAHMS 1911, 57–8, no. 212) – and that between eight and ten skulls were taken out of the broch at Brimsade, Lythmore (Anderson 1890a, 184) – there is a cumulative pattern which suggests that at least some of these human deposits are similar to those recovered from Kettleburn and Hillhead. During his visit to Old Strikoke broch, Anderson (1890a, 143) noted that:

> At the north-east side of the mound there was a pretty extensive refuse heap or kitchen midden, consisting principally of turf or peat ashes, mingled with charred wood, and containing a large admixture of broken and split bones of the usual animals, among which were also portions of a human skull.

Mulville *et al.* (2003) and Armit & Ginn (2007) have demonstrated that during the Middle Iron Age, human remains become more numerous on settlements, with a particular focus on the human head. For example, excavations at Dun Vulan, South Uist uncovered a series of disarticulated remains from throughout the long sequence of occupation (Parker Pearson & Sharples 1999; Mulville *et al.* 2003). Many appear to have been curated and used as foundation deposits. The use of disarticulated remains for foundation 'votive' deposits is also apparent at Cnip, Lewis (Armit & Ginn 2007; Armit 2006).

However, not all human remains were deposited in pits or foundation deposits. Disarticulated human bone, again with a preference for human skulls, was identified in numerous rubble and building contexts, and occasional floor deposits from, for example, Howe, Orkney (Ballin Smith 1994). And the deposits were not always associated with the construction of buildings: many were linked to closure and abandonment. In keeping with the long tradition on the site, disarticulated human remains were associated with the 'closing deposits' at Dun Vulan (see Mulville *et al.* 2003, 24). Additionally, the base of the rubble infill within the complex Atlantic roundhouse at Dun Mor Vaul yielded a disarticulated body, the cranium of which had perhaps been dealt a blow by a sword or an axe (MacKie 1974, 214). At Scalloway, Shetland the head of a woman had been 'squashed between the foundation and the first course of a wall associated with the final rebuilding of the roundhouse' (Sharples 1998, 51). It is possible that this deposition of human bones in settlement contexts could have overlapped with the Pictish burials described later.

So what do these deposits mean?

Armit & Ginn (2007, 127) remind us that 'it is improbable that any single interpretation will be sufficient to explain the occurrence of human remains from Atlantic Scotland in the pre-Pictish period.' They (*ibid.* 123) reasonably argue that disarticulated remains, as a group, are more convincingly votive than articulated burials, and there are few that cannot be interpreted in this light. Although the association of some remains with doorways may suggest a link to the entry and control of buildings, it is more complicated than that. Many deposits were also associated with foundation and abandonment contexts. As Armit & Ginn (2007, 125) highlight, the contexts of the deposition of humans suggest that the rites punctuated the lives of communities and the structures they inhabited. As suggested by the instance of Crosskirk man, the human body may have played an active role during the complete life cycle of a settlement.

There are numerous interpretations for what the actual heads represent, ranging from cannibalism to headhunting, sacrifice to ancestor veneration (Armit & Ginn 2007, 127–30). Irrespective of which interpretation we choose, most modern scholars would reject one suggestion: cannibalism. The reasons for this are sound, but cannibalism as a plausible explanation for the evidence was once in vogue, particularly during the time when the first brochs in Caithness were being excavated. During the excavations undertaken by Rhind and Laing in the 1850s and 1860s the human remains encountered at Kettleburn and Keiss Harbour were discussed under such terms.

In recognising that the child's jawbone discovered at Keiss Harbour was found alongside animal bones that were presumably part of the food chain, Laing & Huxley(1866, 28) concluded that this association, 'raises a strong assumption that these aboriginal savages were occasionally cannibals'. They go on to say (*ibid.* 29):

> I may add in confirmation of the fact of occasional cannibalism that fragmentary human remains have been found in several other refuse heaps in Caithness, and that Professor Owen, whose attention has been specifically directed to the subject, considers that the child's jaw above referred to, has been splintered open precisely in the manner in which animal jaws are frequently opened by human agency to extract the juices of the dentary canal, and not in the way in which a dog or wolf would have gnawed the bone.

Rhind (1853, 217) also ponders whether the skulls from Kettleburn were indicative of cannibalism. Both Laing & Huxley (1866, 29–30) and Rhind (1853, 217) refer to the writings of Diodorus and Strabo who ascribe to the inhabitants of Ireland in the first century AD 'a gastronomic affection for the flesh of their deceased relatives' and to St Jerome who avers, *'ipse viderim Attacottos* [a Scottish tribe] *humanis vesci carnibus'*. Whilst Laing & Huxley (1866, 29–30) use these historical references to bolster their contention for Iron Age cannibalism, Rhind (1853, 217) is more sanguine:

> We must not, however, be hasty in stigmatising a people with the infamy of cannibalism except on the most unquestionable authority: nor would it be logical, far less would it be just, to accuse them of possessing so abominable an appetite on the evidence of one or two isolated facts which may have been purely accidental in origin.

We have to remember that when Rhind excavated Kettleburn broch it was only the second roundhouse on record to have been investigated. Whilst he may still have found the notion of his ancestors being cannibals unpalatable, his opinions would have been influenced by the recovery of human skulls from broch mounds in the following decades, which appeared to compound the idea. Laing also offers another interpretation of the Keiss skull suggesting that 'human flesh may have been eaten under the pressure of famine by races who were not habitual cannibals' (Laing & Huxley 1866, 30). The abundant animal and fish bones, and residues of other foodstuffs that were recovered on almost every subsequent broch excavation obviously counters the suggestion

Fig 7.2 The skull from Hillhead, note the holes in the skull (copyright National Museums Scotland)

that Iron Age peoples were part-time cannibals when other foodstuffs ran dry! The inhabitants of Keiss Harbour had easy access to the sea and to prime agricultural land, which suggests that the recovery of human skulls cannot be taken to mean that the deceased were part of the daily food chain.

Finding the notion of cannibalism, quite literally, too hard to swallow, Rhind (1853, 216) suggested that the skulls were trophies, the heads of slain enemies. He notes that many of the early Celtic nations were addicted to this custom. He refers to Diodorus who talks of the Gauls fastening the heads of the slain to the doors of their houses, as if they were wild beasts captured in hunting (*ibid.* 217). Given the contexts of discovery of the skulls from Hillhead, which had holes bored in their craniums (Fig. 7.2), it seems a sensible interpretation. That said, others have suggested that the purpose of the piercings may have been to let out evil spirits, or to consecrate the deceased by using the symbol of the trinity (author and date unknown, *A Skull Found in Caithness*).

WHITEGATE

During his excavations at Whitegate, Sir Francis Tress Barry recovered human skull fragments (NMS X.GA 606–9). Unfortunately, there is no record of where they were found. One of the skulls has recently been dated to 210–50BC (Tucker & Armit 2009, 215). During re-excavation of Whitegate by the authors, Jon Henderson, and Graeme Cavers, we found a chamber within the roundhouse wall: this chamber was over a metre high and full of animal bone, as well as some human remains. A layer of re-deposited boulder clay sealed this level. On top of the clay were disarticulated human remains, including a skull (Fig. 7.3).

Before we obtained radiocarbon dates we obviously had no idea of the date of these deposits. The deposits were not associated with any other recognisable or dateable

Fig 7.3 The bone deposit at Whitegate being excavated

finds – not a single piece of pottery. In our eyes at least, it seemed unlikely that the deposit would be medieval in date and, unless Tress Barry was a murderer, it was also unlikely that it would date to the nineteenth century. Before any post-excavation investigations, we assumed the deposit dated to the Long Iron Age (first millennium BC to first millennium AD). This was not merely wishful thinking, as the deposit seemed to fit into wider Atlantic Iron Age patterns.

The deposition of animal remains is fairly well attested in Atlantic Scotland, the best example being from Sollas, North Uist, where various species were present in many sub-floor pits. Of approximately 150 pits, some sixty produced material of overtly ritualistic character (Campbell 1991; Armit 1996, 153). Although no human remains were recovered, the deposition of objects in pits also included non-animal remains, such as crucibles and quern stones. Over 37 sites in Atlantic Scotland have now produced evidence of human remains, many disarticulated; of these, many are skull fragments.

The apparent relationship between animal and human remains is an interesting one although direct relationships are fairly uncommon. However, at Hornish Point the disarticulated body of a child was buried in four separate pits. Three of these pits also contained the bones of young animals. An animal skull was buried with a human skull at Cnip (Armit 2006, 134; Armit & Ginn 2007, 122, 130).

Foundation pits usually dominate the archaeological literature, but this is largely the result of a lack of excavations through the structures of buildings. At Cnip wheelhouse, important deposits were found in the walls. Only a short stretch of walling was dismantled during the final days of the excavation, yet a series of discrete deposits was found, including a complete pottery vessel; the head of a great auk; and an articulated portion of cattle vertebrae. This is interpreted as relating to the consecration of the building during its construction and parallels the burial of the boy and accompanying animals at Hornish Point wheelhouse, and the pits at Sollas wheelhouse (Armit 2006, 247). Armit (*ibid.*) is correct in saying that similar wall deposits may exist unnoticed at previously excavated wheelhouse sites, since it is not clear from the published literature that any have previously been dismantled in this way. The same is true of Atlantic roundhouses and brochs. That said, although it is impossible to be sure, it can be suggested that on many sites Barry did not excavate through any wall structure, apart from when he found the entrance to intramural galleries and emptied them out. Thus, the recovery of many of the human remains must have come from the interior: either soil or rubble deposits. Given what we found at Whitegate, it is equally likely that more bodies remain in the walls.

And yes. The radiocarbon dates for the Whitegate bones were Iron Age. They were dated to AD259-432 (Sheridan 2008). This is even more interesting as they broadly date to the same period as some of the human remains from Crosskirk and Hillhead brochs (Tucker & Armit 2009, 215). These emerging patterns strongly suggest that around the 3rd to 5th/6th centuries AD human remains were being deposited on roundhouse sites, presumably long after the period when the roundhouses were first built. The remains, therefore, may pre-date or overlap with other, more formal, burials that have been found in the county, and conventionally labelled 'Pictish'. Let us turn to these remains now.

8. PICTISH BURIALS

GARRYWHIN

As we have already seen, 1866 was a busy year for Joseph Anderson. His obsession with cairns in and around Watenan drew his eye to yet another stony mound, which was 1 metre high and 6 metres in diameter. During his excavations he found a circular, drystone coursed wall. Excavation of the interior revealed another wall and at one end lay the remains of a skeleton, lying on a flat stone. He also found charcoal and pottery. Nearby were four cists, many of which were excavated prior to Anderson's work. Beside two of the cists were small stones, which may have been part of the enclosing cairns that once covered the core cairns (RCAHMS 1911, no. 538, 169–70). Various interpretations have been offered for the structure excavated by Anderson. Curle (RCAHMS 1911, 168) and Close-Brooks (1984, 99) suggested that it was a hut circle. However, Anderson, Edwards (1926, 174) and Ashmore (1980) suggested it was a burial cairn: but of what date?

KEISS AND BIRKLE HILLS

In the very same year as Anderson opened his Garrywhin cairn, Samuel Laing published his book, with co-author T. H. Huxley, *Prehistoric Remains of Caithness* (1866), which recorded his excavations around the north-east bays of Caithness.

Laing was born in Edinburgh, the son of Samuel Laing, a well-known author of books on Norway and Sweden, and nephew of Malcolm Laing, the historian of Scotland. In 1827, he entered St John's College, Cambridge, and, after graduating, he was elected a fellow. He was called to the bar in 1837, and became private secretary to Henry Labouchere, later 1st Baron Taunton, who was then the president of the Board of Trade. In 1842, Samuel was made secretary to the Railway Department and in 1848 was appointed chairman and managing Director of the London, Brighton and South Coast Railway. He became chairman of the Crystal Palace Company in 1852. The same year he was elected to Parliament as a Liberal Party candidate for Wick Burghs. After losing his seat in 1857, he was re-elected in 1859 and appointed financial secretary to the Treasury. In 1860, he became the finance minister of India. On returning from India, he was re-elected to parliament for Wick in 1865 but defeated in 1868. In 1873 he was elected as candidate for Orkney and Shetland, a seat he retained until 1885. As well as his work on the prehistory of Caithness, he also found time to publish a series of books: *Modern Science and Modern Thought* (1885), *Problems of the Future* (1889) and *Human Origins* (1892). Laing died at Sydenham on 6 August 1897.

Laing clearly was a well-respected and academic individual but in the story of Caithness' archaeology he is a curious personality and has a curious reputation.

Laing investigated a range of sites in and around Sinclair's Bay, which were promptly published in his 1866 book. Like all good scholars, Laing outlined his research aims in the opening pages of his book. Boldly, he stated that he wished to find evidence to bridge the gap between the earliest human 'quaternary' occupation and the later 'historic' period (Laing & Huxley 1866, 2). Laing was searching for the 'Pre-historic' period and hoped to see whether there were distinct Stone, Bronze and Iron Age periods of Scotland and, by inference, Britain. Prior to his work he believed that:

'if the case rested solely on British evidence, probably most antiquarians would have been of opinion that there was no sufficient ground for any other hypothesis than that the race found in Britain by the Romans had colonised an unoccupied country a few centuries before the dawn of history' (Laing & Huxley 1866, 3–4).

To elucidate these aims, he had two main targets: middens and burials. By referencing work in Denmark and Switzerland, Laing believed that it was the refuse heaps (i.e. middens) which could throw light on the habits and conditions of the 'prehistoric populations', and that they required the most accurate and systematic investigation, not only to give us truth, but to escape creating error (*ibid.* 4). Laing clearly understood that middens could contain evidence from many periods and realised the importance of finding undisturbed stratigraphy (*ibid.* 5). Burials were also central to Laing's work. He was keen to discover graves and skeletons of the earliest race, ideally connected with middens (Laing & Huxley 1866, 9). Like other contemporaries, he was on the hunt for human remains in an attempt to characterise and better understand the physical features of early peoples. For this, Laing relied heavily on the expertise of Thomas Huxley, then at the height of his fame as Darwin's 'bulldog' (Clarke 2002, 5); and both of Laing's publications (1866; 1868) contain many pages on the human remains. Whilst admitting that he had not entirely fulfilled all of his primary research aims Laing (1866, 9) modestly concluded that he had been 'unexpectedly successful' in some.

His excavation techniques and methodologies were relatively well advanced and on a par with his contemporaries. He placed emphasis on stratigraphic relationships and understanding of taphonomic processes; their importance to him is demonstrated clearly in his excavations at Keiss Harbour broch, where he recognised floors or pavements at different levels, as shown by a series of plans and sections that were drawn up (Fig. 8.1; Laing & Huxley 1866, 23–5, Figs 34–6). He noted that, 'The remarkable fact in this mound is, that it indicated successive occupation, and adaptation of the older parts of the building by newer inhabitants' (*ibid.* 24). Further, he noted that:

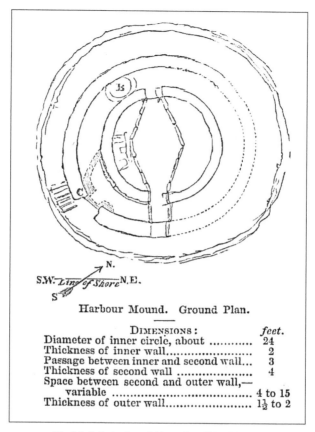

Harbour Mound. Ground Plan.

DIMENSIONS: | feet.
Diameter of inner circle, about 24
Thickness of inner wall........................ 2
Passage between inner and second wall... 3
Thickness of second wall 4
Space between second and outer wall,—
    variable .... 4 to 15
Thickness of outer wall..................... 1½ to 2

Fig 8.1 Laing's plan of his work at Keiss Harbour

There were three distinct middens, separated by superimposed pavements, which, without expressing any theory, and simply as a convenient mode of representing the facts, I may call the primary, secondary, and tertiary middens (*ibid.* 25).

He then went on to list other clear proof of successive occupation from other sources (*ibid.* 25–26).

During his time at Keiss, Laing investigated a number of sites including the broch at Keiss Harbour; a midden, which may be associated with another broch at 'Churchyard Mound'; and a medieval site at Moorland Mound (aka 'the Kirk Stones') (Laing & Huxley 1866; 1868; see also Nicolson 1916). For now though, we are interested in two other sites at Keiss and Birkle Hills.

The mound lay on the southern outskirts of modern day Keiss at the point where the sandy links end and the sand of the seashore changes into rock (Laing & Huxley 1866, 10). Prior to excavation, the site was an irregular mound of sand, half a mile long and situated near the sea (Fig. 8.2; *ibid.* 11). Excavation revealed a remarkable series of cist burials; indeed, Laing notes (*ibid.* 12) that, 'cists were found in every

105

instance with wonderful regularity at about fifteen feet apart, in the central line of the mound'. Initially, Laing suggested that the mound might contain up to 60 cists and could represent the burial place of a surrounding population. Although he refined the number later, he did uncover at least ten cists (see Laing & Huxley 1866, 10–19 for review and Laing 1868 for subsequent work).

All of the cists had the same attributes: they were constructed of unhewn flagstones with no floor, and were covered with large, flat stones. The majority of skeletons were extended and lay in no particular direction. Although most were reclined on their right side there were variations. Some individuals lay face downwards. Also, not everyone was buried in a cist (Laing 1868, 59). In one instance, the cists lay in a double tier, one over the other.

Laing's accounts of other structural details are frustratingly ambiguous. On the one hand he records that, 'above each cist was a small cairn or pile of stones from the beach, from one to three feet high, and above this, one to three feet of sand, covered by turf' (Laing & Huxley 1866, 12–13). In other records he notes that, 'cairns of stones had been piled up over some of the kists, and on others it seems as if a grave mound of sand had been piled up, and some larges stones placed on it' (Laing 1868). That said, as at Garrywhin, there are strong suggestions that some cists, if not all, were covered with stone cairns and/or mounds.

As Laing freely admits, part of his search at Keiss was for a person of superior rank. Believing that this person would be found in the centre of the mound, he cut two trenches across the centre. The northernmost trench discovered 'Kist 7' in which lay the skeleton of a man 'much taller than any of the others previously opened' (1866, 14). Unusually, this grave also contained an object, which Laing (*ibid.*) believed to be a stone celt. Another trench uncovered the 'chief's kist' (Cist 8) which contained 'the skeleton of a tall man of very massive proportions' (*ibid.* 15). Beside him were a series of twelve stone objects, which Laing took to be weapons. The cist was surrounded by a round, horizontally coursed kerb cairn (Fig. 8.3; Laing & Huxley 1866, 15, Figs 6 and 7). A short while after, two other cists were opened in the mound. Apparently, these too contained stone artefacts (Laing 1868, 59).

Laing then headed south, down the shores of Sinclair's Bay to another conspicuous mound in the centre of the bay at Wester. These links were home to two prominent mounds, called Birkle Hills (Fig. 8.4). When Laing visited, small cairns of massive stones could be seen on both mounds. The larger mound turned out to be Wester (or Castle Lingas broch) and need not detain us here. At the base of the smaller mound was another stone cist:

> exactly like those of the [Keiss] burial mound, the head stone which just projected above the sand … It had been opened – I believe a few years ago, by a medical man now in India – but the skeleton, with the exception of the skull, which was wanting, had been replaced in the cist (1866, 31).

Laing discovered three or four other cists of similar construction lying scattered around the base of the small mound; on the west side of the large mound another cist

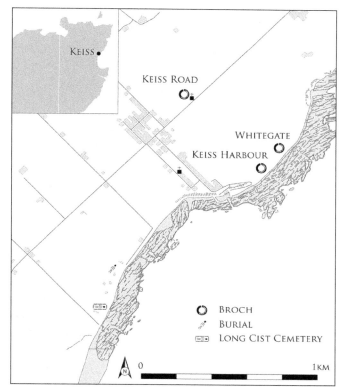

Fig 8.2 Location of the Keiss links burial

containing small fragments of human bones was also found. Laing was adamant that his Birkle and Keiss cists were connected. He notes that they were of the same size and construction and that the stone 'objects' were similar.

In summary, Joseph Anderson's and Laing's excavations around various parts of eastern Caithness uncovered a series of cists some of which could have been associated with stone cairns and kerbs. But what date were they? Who built them?

Laing took up the chronological baton. We have seen that on other burial sites – such as Neolithic chambered cairns and Bronze Age cists – diagnostic artefacts, particularly pottery, allow closer chronological resolution. However, none of the cists uncovered by Anderson or Laing contained pottery; indeed most had no objects at all. Nonetheless, on the basis of the stone items, and his views on evolution, Laing had no hesitation in assigning his cists to the early Stone period. His views did not meet with widespread acceptance. We have already noted that Robert Shearer was scathing in his assessment of Laing's work – but he was not alone. Joseph Anderson was an equally resolute critic. Writing in the *John O' Groat Journal* Anderson concluded:

It is little short of ludicrous to see a few days' antiquarian dilettantism among the sand hills of Keiss brought forward to supply the missing links of European

Fig 8.3 The 'chief's kist' from Keiss

Fig 8.4 Laing's sketch of Birkle Hills

archaeology, and to remodel the whole system of British antiquities. Mr Laing did well in exploring; we cannot say he has done wisely in making a book (Cairnduna 1916).

Anderson was exasperated by Laing's claims to have answered far-reaching issues on the basis of a few days digging. This exasperation was founded on Laing's misidentification of many objects, particularly from the Keiss and Birkle Hill burials. We have noted that the chief's burial contained a range of stone objects which Laing interpreted as a battleaxe, spearheads, an arrowhead, knives and a celt. But many believe that none of these 'objects' are bona fide artefacts (see Close-Brooks, quoted in Ashmore 1980, 349). Anderson had apparently raised these issues with Laing before. Aware of the emerging criticism Laing noted that some individual(s) already had doubts concerning the nature of the artefacts and retorted 'it would be a waste of words to refute such assertions' (Laing 1868, 61).

Anderson was also irked by the way that Laing used the accumulated data to formulate wider interpretations. On the basis of the stone 'artefacts', and more specifically the crudeness of them, Laing assigned both the Keiss and Birkle Hill burials to the early Stone period:

What I think certain is that these people were too rude to have known anything of the arts or metals current among the people of the later Stone or Bronze periods of the Continent and Britain. ... The evidence for this conclusion rests mainly on the weapons buried with the dead. ... An armoury of the most rude and primitive possible forms of spear- and arrow-heads, knives, and hatchets, could hardly have been used by a people who had known, even by tradition, I will not say the use of metals, but even the more advanced forms of stone and bone which are so commonly found throughout Scotland, and in this very district (Laing 1866, 38–40).

He also dismisses the structural parallels of the cists with Early Christian burials noting that none of the Keiss burials faced east–west (*ibid.* 43). He reiterates his point in what we think is one of the most entertaining quotes from the study of Caithness' archaeology:

is there such an irresistible presumption that this most obvious and simple mode of burial could never have been practised previously, as to compel us to admit the most glaring anomalies, such as the existence of a race of rude limpet-eating savages ignorant of metals in the days of St. Columba, in districts which had been for centuries previously the seats of a comparatively civilized people, who reared massive tombs and temples, placed the ashes of the dead in sepulchral urns, and manufactured elegant weapons and ornaments of bronze? ... The theory that all extended kists necessarily show Christian influence, leads to the absurd supposition that the savage who lay in the extended kist at Keiss, with his rude stone weapons by his side, and a handful of limpets for his food in another world, may have been the identical prince who visited the Court of Scotland, conversed with St. Columba, and entertained his missionaries (*ibid.* 45–6).

Laing's early date was not only confined to the cist burials, he reserved the same interpretation for the brochs and middens he uncovered (Laing & Huxley 1866, 22–30, 61). When referring to the unnamed individuals who suggested that the relics from these sites, and the graves, might be of a later date, Laing (*ibid.* 41–2) stated:

To suppose, as some have done, that these relics may be as recent as the Christian era, is to cut away from under our feet all possible ground for archaeological classification. It is undoubted that the Romans found Caledonia inhabited by races acquainted with iron, and possessing sufficient civilization and capacity for military and political organization, to oppose a formidable resistance to the legions of Agricola. What likelihood is there, that a people worse armed than the savages of the Andamans could have lived in the open defenceless plains of Caithness in contact with such races? ... If the limpet-eating savages, with their rude sandstone knives, lived in these regions until the Christian era, the classification of the Copenhagen Museum must be inverted, and the sepulchral urns and finished ornaments of the Bronze period assigned to an earlier date than the rude implements of the Kjökkenmöddings.

With Rhind's views on the chronology of brochs, published a decade before, firmly in his mind Laing crystallised his thoughts (*ibid.* 56–60):

These burgs ... have usually been assigned to a very recent period ... [but] it seems difficult to believe that such forts could have been built by the limpet-eating savages, whose tools and weapons were ruder than those of the caverns of Les Eyzies or the drifts of Abbeville. And yet such seems to be the evidence of the section of the Harbour Mound ... there is a good deal of evidence to show that the burgs really date back to a very remote period. ... On the whole, therefore, I see no difficulty in assigning a high antiquity to many of these burgs, and considering these primitive structures to have been the work of the people, whoever they were, who reared the Stones of Stenness ... long prior to the general introduction of metals or the advent of any historical race.

Laing restated his position two years later (1868, 62), 'the original inhabitants of the burg at Keiss must have been rude savages, anterior to the comparatively civilised people of the bronze period'.

Again, Laing turns to the artefactual record to support his claims. He notes that the objects from Keiss Harbour, found in different levels, particularly the middens, were essentially distinct. Bone and pottery were exclusively found in the lower middens and the few instances of metallic objects, finer pottery, and well-wrought bone implements were confined to the upper middens. In attempting to understand how such 'primitive' people could have built such impressive stone structures it is worth quoting extensively from Laing & Huxley (1866, 60–1):

The sandstone of the district gave a material so bad for cutting purposes that the weapons and tools of the primitive savages, and all arts and ornaments depending on cutting tools, remained at the lowest ebb; while on the other hand Nature provided a boundless profusion of flags and blocks regularly squared for building. ... I have often thought that the instinct of children affords some clue to that of savages; and on these shores I have seen children, tempted by the facility of selecting stones of regular form, build in sport very substantial miniature round towers, of a form not unlike that of the ancient burgs. In fact, the solid circular tower is a simple idea which could hardly fail to occur to a people, however savage, who felt the want of shelter and defence, and had plenty of squared blocks and flags ready to their hand. ... Such a people might build solid towers while they remain ignorant of fish-hooks and barbed arrow-heads, and never attempted to carve ornaments on the handles of their knives or lances.

And who were these savages who were buried in the cists and populated brochs?

It is a most important and interesting fact that in association with these very rude and primitive remains a type of human race should have been discovered so savage and degraded, as to present more resemblance to the lowest Australian than to any historical European race. ... Now in all these particulars the type [of skull], of which the Caithness skull No. 1 is the extreme example, is far more animal-like than that of any European race either known in history or hitherto discovered in prehistoric tombs of the Iron, Bronze, or later Stone periods. ... No one can doubt that we have here an extremely savage type ... [who] lived on for an indefinite period little changed, until they were exterminated, or enslaved and assimilated, by superior races in times approaching to the historical era ... The whole story would then be consistent – strangeness and extreme rudeness of weapons and implements would correspond with strangeness and extreme rudeness of human type (*ibid.*, 62–4).

Although Laing noted that at least one of the Keiss skeletons was a 'fair specimen of an ancient Briton differing in no essential respect from a modern European' (*ibid.* 64) he suggests that the majority of the skulls were those of savages. The more 'civilised skulls' were either evidence of accidents, particularly shipwrecks whereby a few isolated individuals of superior race were thrown up on the shores of Caithness (*ibid.* 66–7), or superior races occasionally mingling with the Caithness savages (*ibid.* 71).

It goes without saying that these interpretations completely clashed with Rhind and Anderson. Laing could not have had a more diachronic view of the world. Laing saw graves and brochs within the Stone Age, whereas Anderson (1890a, 152–3) saw them as Iron Age, perhaps even post-dating the Roman period (1883, 258–9). Laing saw brochs as being of a simple design, whereas Anderson (*ibid.* 1890a, 150) believed that, 'the period of the brochs must necessarily have been one of very great importance in the early history of Scotland. No other period in that history surpasses it in the number and magnitude of its structural remains.'

ACKERGILL

A few decades after his spat with Laing, Joseph Anderson returned to Caithness to visit Sir Francis Tress Barry who was excavating a series of brochs in and around Sinclair's Bay. During his 1896 visit to Barry's residence at Keiss Castle, Anderson was shown an ogham-inscribed Pictish symbol stone (Fig 1.12). The stone, incised on one face, depicts the lower part of a fish and a rectangular symbol, which is divided and decorated with spirals and is possibly a comb-case. The ogham inscription has been read as 'NEHTETRI' and translated as 'Neht, son of Etrios'. The stone was brought to Barry by John Nicolson, who had found it lying exposed in several fragments on the south side of the links of Keiss Bay (Allen & Anderson 1903, 28).

Two decades later, during conversation with Mrs Duff-Dunbar, who was one of Anderson's successors at the National Museum of Antiquities, Arthur Edwards discovered that the Pictish stone originally stood at the north-west end of another natural, elongated, sandy mound locally known as Ackergill (Edwards 1926, 161; Fig. 1, 179). It should be noted that at the start of the twentieth century, Sinclair's Bay was known locally as the Keiss estate, therefore we cannot assume that every object labelled 'Keiss Links' came from the immediate area in and around modern day Keiss. Ackergill is a real possibility for the find spot of the Pictish stone.

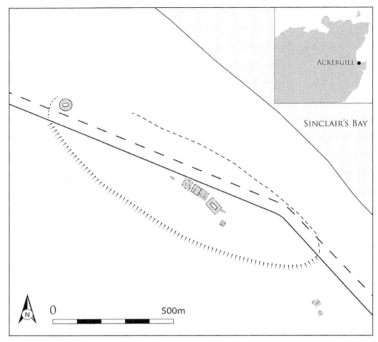

Fig 8.5 Location of Ackergill graves

Ackergill Links sits at the southern end of Sinclair's Bay and is dominated by a series of sandy mounds. Together with Keiss and Birkle Hills it forms a perfect arc of natural mounds running the length of the bay's curvature (Fig. 8.5). In 1902 John Nicolson painted and sketched a series of drawings, which he annotated Ackergill. They appear to show cist burials, some of which are surrounded by arcs of stones which may be the remains of kerb cairns (Fig. 8.6). There appears to have been another cist mound on Sinclair's Bay, which was possibly associated with those uncovered by Edwards (see also Ritchie 2011).

In the 1920s, quantities of human bones were recovered from the area when a road was built through the mound and this prompted Edwards, then the assistant keeper of the National Museum of Antiquities, to undertake the first, and only, organised excavation of the mound in 1925 and 1926. Like Keiss, the Ackergill mound is expansive: it measures more than 100 metres in length. Although Edwards only excavated a small part of the mound, he found burials at both of its extremities, which suggested that – like Keiss – Ackergill was a significant cemetery.

During his two seasons of excavations Edwards discovered a series of burials: at least two isolated cists (Graves 1 and 7), seven square or rectangular cairns (Graves 2–5, 8–10), and a circular cairn (Grave 6). He also uncovered another Pictish symbol stone fragment (see Blackie & Macaulay 1998, 8–9). This site is critical in attempting to understand the remains found previously by Anderson and Laing and we make no apology for discussing Edward's findings in greater, or some may argue cumbersome, detail (also see Ritchie 2011).

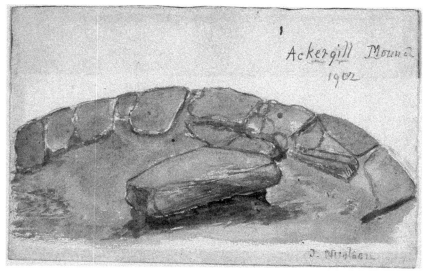

Fig 8.6 Nicolson's 1902 sketch of Ackergill Mound (copyright RCAHMS)

The isolated cists: Graves 1 and 7

Two isolated cists (Graves 1 and 7; Fig. 8.7) were recovered. The first (1) was a long cist with no associated stone cairn. It had perhaps been disturbed prior to his investigation, as it was filled with sand; near the bottom, Edwards uncovered a number of the long bones and ribs of a human skeleton, but no skull (*ibid.* 162). The aforementioned Pictish stone was found near the head end of the cist. The second isolated cist (Grave 7) contained the remains of a woman, fully extended and lying face down. There is reason to suppose that these two cists were broadly contemporary with those found under the rectangular cairns (see below): not only were they similar, but they also lay on the line of the cemetery (see also Ashmore 1980, 348).

The square cairns: Graves 2–5, 8–10

Edwards uncovered seven square or rectangular cairns, four during the first season (Graves 2–5) and three the following season (Graves 8–10) (Fig. 8.8). Moving eastwards from Grave 1, Edwards noticed that the upper portions of the stones of another long cist (Grave 2) were showing above a mass of pebbles and small stones. The cist contained a few long bones, the vertebrae of a human skeleton and, at the north-west end, some fragments of skull. The cist was set within a kerb (stones placed on their flat surfaces as to form a kerb – perhaps suggesting horizontal coursing) and three of the corners had upright stones. The space between the kerb and the cist was filled in with water-worn stones from the beach.

Grave 3, another square cairn, lay less than a metre away. Again, it had a horizontally coursed kerb and, again, at each of the four corners a single stone was set on end. The interior was filled with a mass of pebbles and stones, and the uppermost layer consisted mainly of white quartzite pebbles. Below this level was a layer of larger stones

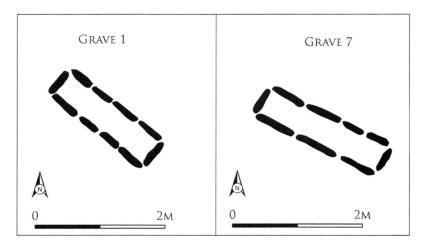

Fig 8.7 The isolated cists: Graves 1 & 7, Ackergill

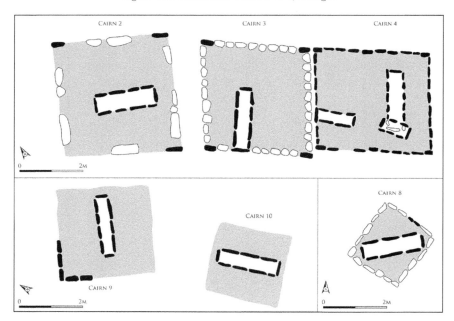

Fig 8.8 The square cairns: Graves 2, 3, 4, 8, 9 & 10, Ackergill

and finally at the bottom, resting on sand, a stratum of still larger water-worn stones and boulders (*ibid.* 164). During his first fieldwork season, Edwards found neither an associated cist nor any trace of remains (*ibid.*, 162, Fig. 2). However, when he revisited the grave in 1926, 4 feet below the bottom of the kerb, in undisturbed sand, a cist was found (Edwards 1927, 198). The cist was not central: the south-western end lay almost in line with the bottom of the kerb. It contained the remains of a woman, fully extended and lying on her back.

Grave 4 was also a square cairn. Unlike Grave 3 it had a kerb made from vertical slabs set on edge (as opposed to horizontal coursing). Again – except in the north-west, where a stone was missing – an upright stone marked each corner. However, upright stones were also placed in the middle of some kerbs, as if to mark a notional centre. Again, the uppermost levels of the cairn consisted of small quartzite pebbles and below these were a number of larger stones intermixed with larger pebbles of quartzite. When these layers were removed two cists (A and C) were uncovered. Another cist (B) was discovered later, at a lower level. Cist A was unusual, in that it had a cist within a cist. The upper cist held the remains of a young infant of 16 to 20 months old. The body had been placed on its back, fully extended, with the head at the north-west end. Immediately below this cist was another cist (B) which contained the skeleton of a middle-aged man lying on his back, fully extended, his arms placed under his buttocks. His skull had been moved and was found lying near the right side of his chest. The final cist within Grave 4 (C) had been disturbed; the skull had a few bones lying beside it, but many bones were missing. The remains appeared to be that of an eight-year-old.

Grave 8 was another square cairn, with a kerb constructed of horizontal coursing and stones set on edge. As with Grave 3, at first it did not appear that there was a cist; Edwards had to dig down more than five feet to find the cist (Edwards 1927, 198). The cist contained the skeleton of a man, who was found lying on his back, fully extended, with his head at the west end.

Graves 9 and 10 were found in a mound situated a little further to the south-east of the larger mound. Only part of the kerb of Grave 9 remained and the overlying covering of boulders was scattered. Edwards' (1927, 197, Fig. 2) plan suggests that the surviving kerb was constructed of upright stones. The skeleton of a woman was found; she was on her back, fully extended, with her head at the south-west end.

Grave 10 had no kerb or enclosing structure, and consisted only of an upper covering layer of boulders. Two cists were discovered beneath the boulders: one was superimposed on the other, with the floor of the uppermost cist acting as the cover for the lower. No fragments of bones or any other objects were found in the upper cist; the lower cist contained the skeleton of a man, who was on his back, fully extended, with his head at the south end.

The rectangular cairn: Grave 5

Near to Grave 4 was Grave 5 (Fig. 8.9). Again, the corners were marked, as were the middles of the long kerb sides. The cairn had been made with great care.

First a layer of stones had been placed on their flat faces in the sand; above these successive layers of similar stones had then been placed in such a manner that each overlapped the other in a scale-like fashion. Above this was another layer of rounded water-worn stones, and covering all, a layer of from 6 to 9 inches in depth of smooth white pebbles of quartzite, which varied in size from that of the egg of a pigeon to that of an ostrich. The layer of pebbles covered the upper surface of the wall only, and did not extend over the actual chamber. The inner faces of this thick wall which formed the sides and ends of the chamber measured 1 foot 6 inches in height, and were composed of large stones laid prostrate as to form a

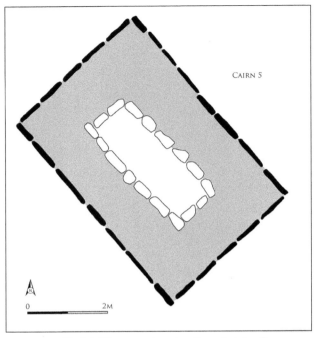

Fig 8.9 The rectangular cairn: Grave 5, Ackergill

regular facing. The actual number of courses was six, each of which projected a little inwards from the one below, so as to make the sides converge slightly (Edwards 1926, 168).

Although Grave 5 had some structural similarities with the other graves, there were subtle differences. First, it was rectangular, as opposed to square. Second, the cairn comprised a seemingly well built chamber, which housed two burials (D and E), a male and a female, one separated from the other by a row of upright flags set on edge. Each part formed a separate cist over which cover stones had been placed. Edwards noted (*ibid.*) that, 'it seemed on the whole as if much greater care had been taken in the burial of D, that of the male, than in E, that of the female'. The male skeleton, whose skull closely resembled that from Grave 4 (B), lay on his back, fully extended, with his head to the north-west. The female was elderly and lay on her left side – fully extended, with her face down – but in the opposite direction to the male, her head to the south-east. The male grave was paved, the female one was not.

The circular cairn: Grave 6

Two hundred feet away from the aforementioned cluster, Edwards uncovered another cairn – but this time it was circular (Fig. 8.10). Although no pebbles were found on the sides or top of the actual structure, Edwards did uncover a large number of white quartzite pebbles near the kerb on the south-east side, which had probably fallen from the sloping sides of the structure.

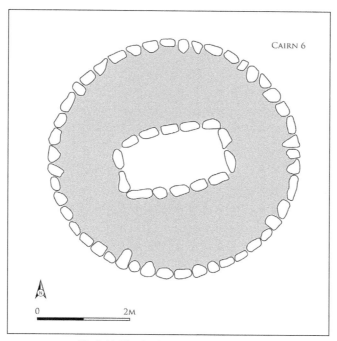

Fig 8.10 The circular cairn: Grave 6, Ackergill

The cairn contained a well built corbelled chamber, which was filled with sand. In contrast to the other graves, there was no sign of any cists. Within the sandy fill, four skeletons were recovered. The first, an adolescent female a little over 20 years of age (Skeleton F), was lying fully extended on her left side, with her head facing downwards; A bronze chain adorned her neck. Nearby was the skeleton of a well-developed man of middle age (Skeleton G), who was found lying on his left side in a crouched position. Between these two skeletons, but at a lower level, were the remains of a young person, who was aged about 15 years (Skeleton H) and lay, fully extended, on his/her back. The skull was missing but this may have been removed in modern times during the construction of a signpost. An elderly man, some bones showing signs of rheumatoid arthritis (Skeleton J), was found in the centre of the chamber at floor level.

At Ackergill we have, arguably, one of the most important Early Medieval cemetery sites in northern mainland Scotland. The work done there illustrated again the different ways in which individuals were buried and, more specifically, the variety of ways in which cist burials were used, covered and adorned. In every sense, Edward's findings confirmed, elucidated and illustrated the previous work at Keiss, Birkle and, perhaps, Garrywhin. As seen at Keiss and Birkle Hills, solitary cists were uncovered with no cairns. Contrastingly, other cists were covered with stone cairns, the majority with carefully defined kerbs. As at Keiss, cists were often found in association with other cists: for example, sitting directly on top of one another.

117

Since Anderson's, Laing's and Edwards' excavations, archaeological discussions have focussed on trying to place the architectural remains within a wider chronological framework. Since the 1920s numerous excavations of similar cairns have taken place across Scotland which, together with the results produced by radiocarbon dating of the skeletons, have led to a general consensus that they are Pictish in date (see Ashmore 1980; Close-Brooks 1984). This is supported by the recovery of Pictish stones in and around the areas of cairn excavation. We have already mentioned the two symbol stones from Ackergill, but the link is even stronger. In 1895, Sir Francis Tress Barry donated another Pictish symbol stone from Sinclair's Bay to the National Museum of Antiquities (Donations, *Proc. Soc. Antiq. Scot.*, 1895, 272–4). It was 'found on the smaller of the two sandhills known as Birkle Hills, at the mouth of the Water of Wester, on the estate of Keiss' (*ibid.* 272). This was, of course, the mound excavated by Laing where he discovered various cists. The stone was reused as a paving slab in a rectilinear structure (*ibid.* 273) and although there is no definitive evidence for a relationship with the burial mound, it is a distinct possibility. This association between cists, cairns and symbol stones is lent further credence by a more recent recovery, with which we go full circle and return to where we started: to the area in and around Garrywhin. Half a kilometre from the cairn excavated by Anderson, fragments of another Class I Pictish stone were recovered in 1977. Fieldwork revealed that the largest fragment lay beside a round cairn, over a neat horizontally coursed slab kerb, probably constructed for the purpose of burial. Although not excavated, this site is taken to be a Pictish grave (Ashmore 1980; Gourlay 1984). Recent work by Ritchie (2011, 134–6) confirms the notion that these graves are Pictish in date.

As well as accepting a Pictish date for these sites, most authorities believe that the numerous features contained within the individual sandy mounds are broadly contemporary (Edwards 1926, 172; Ashmore 1980, 348). But not everyone agrees. When discussing the findings from Ackergill, Close-Brooks (1984, 97) suggests that we would do well to bear in mind the possibility that the round cairn may be of a different date to the rectangular cairns. Moreover, she believes that the bronze necklace found within the cairn is similar to one from the Roman fort at Newstead (NMS X.FRA 965), and may, therefore, date to the first or second century AD. Whilst this is a possibility, it is perhaps instructive that some sites outwith the county, for example, Lundin Links, Fife, have a variety of burial customs: cists without monuments/cairns; cists under rectangular cairns; and those under circular cairns, that appear to be contemporary with each other (Greig, Greig & Ashmore 2000).

Whilst it is all very well to be able to suggest a chronological framework for the burial mounds at Keiss and Ackergill, we should not close the pages on these structures just yet. There are many, many more avenues to be explored (see also Ritchie 2011). As we have said in previous sections, past discussions of many Caithness sites have focussed on structures and chronologies. Seldom are other areas considered and this is particularly true of many studies that investigate death in various periods. Analysis of burials is largely descriptive and seldom are other forms of evidence considered. For example, often, the actual people buried in the graves, and their associated goods, are ignored. And again, when individuals and grave goods are considered, discussions are usually descriptive and related to typology and chronology. Additionally, the burials are usually studied in isolation – seldom is their wider geographical and/or chronological location and perspective considered. Perhaps more importantly, however, the active individuals and groups who took part in these mortuary practices are ignored. We must remember that the dead do not bury themselves. It was the living who disposed of the dead. It was the living who built the burial chambers and deposited grave goods with the dead. It was the living who held ceremonies and remembered the dead. When studying death we are equally studying life. Burials tell us as much about the attitudes, values and choices of the living as they do about the deceased. For this reason, it is worth considering the Caithness Pictish burials with fresh eyes. Let us consider again the two burial mounds, at Keiss and Ackergill.

When discussing his findings at Keiss, Laing concluded that:

> The number and regularity of the kists preclude the idea of a hurried interment of bodies slain in battle; and some of the skeletons being of women, confirms the supposition that it was the regular burying-place of a surrounding population (Laing & Huxley 1866, 13).

Analysis of the deceased excavated by Edwards at Ackergill illustrates a mixture of individuals. Six were men, one was advanced in life, the other five died in their prime. Five were women, one was elderly, another middle-aged, and three were females under the age of twenty-five. Two of the bodies were children under 15 years of age, and one was an infant of 16 to 20 months. Although all the burials were inhumations they were found variously on their back, front, or left side. Intriguingly, all of the bodies lying face down were women, although not all women were placed this way. Unlike similar cemetery sites, such as Lundin Links, Fife (Greig, Greig & Ashmore 2000; Williams 2007), the cists and cairns at Ackergill were afforded to all ages.

There can be little doubt then that Keiss and Ackergill were significant foci for the burial of a variety of peoples and ages and could, legitimately, be called cemeteries. In Laing's and Edwards' time these sandy mounds were huge, prominent features in the landscape. They would have been visible during, and long after, some or all of the cists were constructed and covered. They would have been places where people came not only to bury the recently deceased but also to remember their ancestors. The placing of the cairns with no intercuttings is particularly notable and suggests a sense of organisation, order and respect for pre-existing monuments. We have argued previously that the creation of burial monuments in specific places allowed opportunities for the creation of histories and the upholding of ideology and cultural identity at varying social and geographical levels. As Artelius and Svanberg (2005, 5) remind us, the material remains of burial rituals – the graves, the monuments and burial grounds – are assemblages of collective social memories set in relation to a specific physical as well as mental space: the land, the dead and history. Burial monuments and/or landscapes allowed opportunities for individuals and communities to remember their dead in subsequent years. The burial, perhaps even the individuals, kept on living, at least in social memory.

One of the most intriguing things about Ackergill was the extensive use of white quartz pebbles in the cairn constructions. Edwards (1926, 172) noted that whilst Graves 4 and 5 showed the greater evidence for the use of white quartzite pebbles, 'it can safely be assumed that this was a common feature to all'. What does this mean? A visit to the Sinclair's Bay foreshore today demonstrates that picking up, presumably thousands, of white quartzite pebbles would not have been easy; Edwards (1926, 173) himself noted that, 'one might search the whole of the beach in vain for a single specimen of a rounded pebble of white quartzite'.

But gather them in their thousands they did. Perhaps this gathering was a symbolic, communal activity undertaken by the individuals and communities who buried the deceased. Perhaps, in some way, it represented a token of respect in the way that today we leave flowers at a graveside. Indeed, it may well be that the pebbles were deposited over many years, a reverential gift to the deceased. Importantly, as the pebble mound grew it would have glistened in the landscape, a permanent reminder of the deceased. Indeed, the recurrent position of the burial mounds on a sea-facing shelf would have made them striking landmarks for individuals and groups travelling to Sinclair's Bay by boat. However, this is not unique to this site. Williams (2007, 158) convincingly argues that the seaboard setting at Lundin Links would have facilitated an expanded visual experience of the cemetery, from land and sea. Therefore, although the primary intention was that the cairns were to be viewed from a close distance by groups of people, these monuments were also larger symbols in the wider landscape. The need for symbols and markers may also explain why Pictish symbol stones have been found in the immediate locale.

And we may push the story further. There appear to be two or three main types of cist structure: isolated cists with no obvious mound covering; cists with square cairns; and cists with round cairns. But why was this? Why did some cists have no covering? Why were some cairns circular whilst others were square? Is it instructive that the circular cairns are geographically separate from their right-angled neighbours? And why were two graves (5 and 6) chambered? Why did the circular cairn not contain any cists, the bodies merely thrown in the sand at different levels? Does the recovery of bodies at different levels within the sand suggest the deposition of different bodies at different times? Given that there were no chambers or entrances to the cairns, this must mean that either the chamber was left open for a period, hence the sandy fill, or that the chamber was periodically reopened from the top. This may be true of the other cairns with evidence for multiple burials. Indeed, what do the multiple burials tell us? Grave 4 had three cists, but A and C were higher in the cairn than B. Cist A contained the skeleton of a young infant, cist C contained the skull of an eight-year-old. The lowest cist (B) contained a middle-aged male, his skull supposedly moved to the right side of his chest. The infant's cist lay directly on top of the adult males. Edwards explains these findings in a very prosaic way:

Possibly the reason for this [the skull of the man being moved] was, that when the burial of the child took place, which must have been some considerable time after the interment in Cist B, the perhaps unsuspected burial of the adult had been discovered, and the skull pushed forward, as the slab, which now formed the paving-stone of the child's cist, had formerly been one of the cover-stones for that of the adult (Edwards 1926, 167).

Edwards' own drawings show that the child's burial sat directly on top of the man's burial, suggesting that there was not a significant time lag. Could Grave 4 have been a family burial with, perhaps, the male dying first and then the children buried thereafter? If so, why remove the head? The same explanation could, perhaps, be offered for Grave 5. As you will remember, the cairn contained the body of a male, whose skull closely resembled that from Cist B in Grave 4. The other skeleton is of an elderly female. But why are they facing opposite directions? And why is the woman face down?

What does all this diversity mean? The locations, variations in structure, the dead, the grave goods and orientation, the possible later internments within the same cairns, the use of white quartzite pebbles and the recovery of Pictish stones in the area are surely telling us something fundamental about the way burial rites were used by the living to convey social messages. Although we do not have to align ourselves with Laing's suggestion that 'big'='chief', he is surely right when he suggests some form of social distinction. There are many questions to be asked. We need to broaden our analyses away from structural typologies and chronologies. Otherwise we are no further on in our understandings than Anderson and Laing were 120 years ago.

9. WAGS

During his excavations at Yarrows broch Anderson uncovered a series of outbuildings (Fig. 9.1). Two, marked C and D, were curious, long, irregularly shaped enclosures remarkable for the way in which standing stones were set around their interiors at varying distances. Anderson suggested that these outbuildings were later than the broch (Anderson 1890a, 136–7). A few decades later, during his survey of the county, Alexander Curle (1866–1955) recognised similar constructions with peculiar galleries, particularly in the south-eastern area of the county.

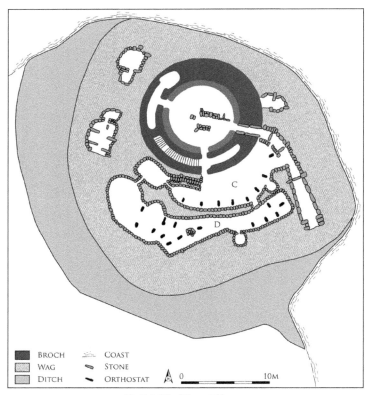

Fig 9.1 The Wags at Yarrows

Alexander Curle is yet another central figure in the story of Caithness' archaeology. His 1910 survey of the monuments of the county remains the cornerstone of any understanding of the county's archaeology. This remarkable piece of work, documented in a journal written by Curle, shows that he visited the majority of the 597 monuments then known over a period of five months from May to September (RCAHMS MS/36/2). The completion of the fieldwork and publication in little more than a year was a staggering achievement (Davidson & Henshall 1991, 8). Like others before him, Curle's reputation goes well beyond the Caithness borders. He is the only person to have held the senior position in three Scottish institutions: as secretary of the RCAHMS; as director of the National Museum of Antiquities of Scotland; and finally as director of the Royal Scottish Museum (Ritchie 2002, 19). His interest in archaeology may have been fired by his father's acquaintance with Anderson (see Ritchie 2002, 20–1). Indeed, when Curle left the RCAHMS to join the National Museum of Antiquities, it was to become Anderson's replacement.

Unsurprisingly, during his Caithness survey the county's rich archaeological remains intrigued and stimulated Curle. He was interested both in excavating a few site types in the hope of obtaining details of their plan, and in recovering relics that might throw light on the question of their period of occupancy. Thus, intermittently, Curle carried out a number of important excavations in Caithness over four decades. One site type he was particularly interested in were the aisled buildings first discussed by Anderson or, as they would later become known, 'wags'.

LANGWELL

The first wag Curle investigated was at Langwell in 1910 (Curle 1912). He revealed a large circular structure, perhaps a hut circle, with an attached galleried structure, or wag (Fig. 9.2). The wag was oblong in plan and measured around 16 metres in length. The building was entered from within the hut circle and it curved around the exterior wall. The wag had rounded ends and was divided internally by a cross wall that was fitted with a doorway. The inner part of this subdivided area had three upright stones (or orthostats) set into the ground on each side of the centre of the structure, which formed a central nave and two side-aisles. The roof had been formed of large slabs with one end on the wall head and the other supported on the upright pillar stones.

WAG OF FORSE

During his subsequent time at the National Museum of Antiquities and the Royal Scottish Museum, Curle's interests in Scottish archaeology focussed mainly outwith Caithness. Between 1910 and 1937 Curle excavated some of the key Scottish archaeological sites at Mote of Mark, Kirkcudbrightshire (Curle 1914), Traprain Law, East Lothian (e.g. Curle & Cree 1916) and Jarlshof, Shetland (Curle 1932; 1933; 1934). After a break of almost three decades, he returned to the county to excavate the Viking settlement of Freswick in 1937 (Curle 1939). When he returned to the county he was

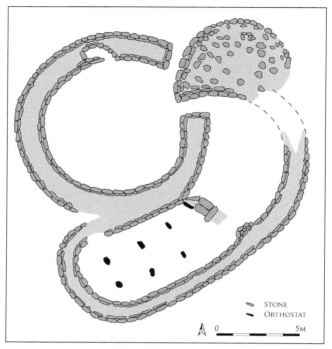

Fig 9.2 Langwell wag

71 years old; given his stage of life – an age when most people would batten down the hatches – we must ask what drove Curle to return to the area. We will have cause to return to this theme later but one answer surely lies in his interest in the Viking period. He moved seamlessly from one Viking settlement (Jarlshof) to another (Freswick) and his general interest in the Viking period might have been heightened by his recording of a possible boat burial at Huna. The finds included timber, rivets, a chain and metal objects (NMRS MS 28/ SAS 461, 20–1; Batey 1984, 58). Yet Curle's interest in Vikings did not erase his interest in wags. Curle continued his work in Caithness until he was 81 years old, excavating at the Wag of Forse (Curle 1941; 1946; 1948). Indeed, it was during his excavations at Freswick in 1937 and 1938 that he made his plans to explore at Forse, and commenced work in June 1939.

We will come to the archaeology in a moment. But for us, any discussion or mention of the Wag of Forse, conjures up one key personality: Meg Sinclair. Meg is the manager of the Dunbeath Heritage Centre and was on the board of CAT. Like many others we have met through this journey, she is passionate about – and is a strong advocate of – the county's archaeology. The Dunbeath Heritage Centre, run by the Dunbeath Preservation Trust, is located in the former school where the famous Scottish writer Neil M. Gunn began his education. It houses an extensive archive of the author's work and an impressive exhibition depicting the lives of the people of Dunbeath over the last 6000 years. There is a wealth of information on the area's archaeology, wildlife and genealogy and it is a crucial stop in any tour of northern Scotland. The reason it

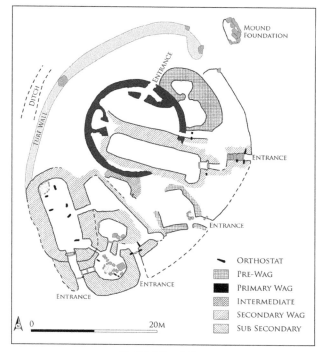

Fig 9.3 Wag of Forse

is one of the best museums in Scotland lies in the vigour of the Trust. Also in the area is one of the best-preserved brochs in the county and the probable Early Christian chapel site at Ballachly, which was recently excavated by another friend of the county, Lloyd Laing.

The Forse estate comprises an incredibly rich archaeological landscape, spanning a period from the Bronze Age to post-medieval times. The multi-period landscape houses deserted farmsteads, field systems, small cairns, hut circles, brochs and burnt mounds (Fig. 9.3; see Mercer 1980, 1981, 1985). But for now, we are interested in the wags, from which the site gets its name.

Although known as the Wag of Forse, the site has many more components than the wags. Baines (1999, 79–80) has recently reviewed the site. The sequence appears to start with several simple round or oval stone-built structures. These were overlain and largely destroyed by a later circular structure which some people (e.g. Baines 1999) believe to be a broch. Others (e.g. MacKie 2007, 438) believe that it is another form of roundhouse, possibly a dun. This large structure stood in an oval enclosure defined by a turf wall with a shallow outer ditch. It may have been surrounded by a number of outer buildings, although this is not clear. The roundhouse was in turn replaced and partially overlain by a collection of wags. At a later stage, a pair of interconnected sub-circular houses were built. Additionally, there are likely to be unexcavated structures within the complex. The present appearance of the site makes it only possible to unravel part of the story.

What the wags were used for is debatable. Curle, in **RCAHMS** (1911) originally labelled the sites galleried 'dwellings' but later suggested that this definition is misleading, preferring to view them as folds for cattle, sheep or other stock (1941, 23, 33). During his excavations of the wags at Forse, Curle mentions the recovery of only a few pieces of pottery and a small number of finds, including hammerstones and abraded pebbles (Baines 1999, 80). No pottery or food refuse was located at the Langwell wag and the few finds included a rotary quern and a saddle quern (Curle 1912, 80–84). No primary hearths were located at either site. Curle, therefore, may be correct in his assertion. The date of the wags is equally puzzling, although a post-broch date is preferred. Thus, wags may contrast with other Early Historic building types and could represent a new architectural form, where aspects of domestic practice that had formerly been contained in a single building – such as storage of food – were divided between separate spaces.

10. VIKING BURIALS

> Caithness was a great Celtic beach on which the Norse wave broke. In the ebb and flow of almost five centuries two great cultures clashed and mingled. Throughout the Viking age and beyond, this area, so often regarded as remote and peripheral was actually at the centre of a world which extended beyond the frontiers unimagined before the Viking expansion (Cowan 1982, 25).

Based on the earliest contemporary historical sources, Viking activity in Scotland has traditionally been dated to around the turn of the 9th century. This was the period of the earliest Viking raids – for example, on Lindisfarne in AD 793; on 'all the islands in Britain' (probably the Hebrides) in AD 794: and on both Rathlin Island and the Isle of Skye in AD 795 (see Barrett 2003, 75–8; Graham-Campbell & Batey 1998, 1–3). Despite these useful documents, there are virtually no contemporary records that mention other parts of Britain and Ireland. In a Scottish context there are no mentions of Orkney, Shetland and Caithness. This lack of written record presents a problem in recognising and dating the establishment of the first Norse settlements in Scotland. The evidence for the period of initial Viking incursions (*c.*9th century) is surprisingly slight. The surviving evidence, particularly from graves and artefacts, suggests that the earliest dating we have in the county is around the tenth century. The limited number of excavated settlements date to after this period.

There are three main non-archaeological sources available in the study of Viking and Late Norse Caithness: the place names, the saga evidence and the historical documentary sources. It is important to note that any review of Viking Caithness has to begin and end with the work of Colleen Batey. As well as undertaking one of the most important programmes of surveys and excavations in the county she has also published a remarkable number of publications. For a useful summary of the nature of the evidence, we strongly advise reading some, if not all, of her work. For now, we acknowledge her work through pointing you to her numerous review articles (e.g. Batey 1987a; 1987b; 1989; 1991a; 1991b) and these and others form the basis of what follows.

The Gaelic and Norse elements in the place-name record appear mutually exclusive indicating a concentration of Scandinavian influence in the north-east of the modern county, with the more indigenous population more restricted inland (Fig. 10.1). The parish of Canisbay has a particular wealth of Norse place names: virtually all names

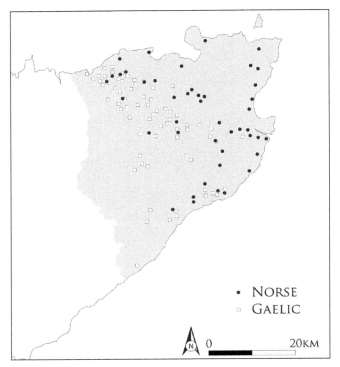

- NORSE
- GAELIC

N   0   20KM

Fig 10.1 Gaelic and Norse place names of Caithness

in the parish can be identified as Norse. This seems to suggest a total suppression of all place names from the pre-Norse period (Batey 1987b, 17).

The earliest dateable reference to Caithness in the Orkneyinga Saga is dated to *c*.AD 874; this tells of an alliance between Earl Sigurd and Thorstein the Red, which resulted in the conquering of 'all Caithness and much more of Scotland, and Moray and Ross'. Other sources seem to indicate that Vikings were already established in Orkney before coming to Caithness, and that after the victory many settled in the area (see Batey 1987b, 19). There are various references to Caithness in the saga literature, and the author may even have stayed in Caithness at some point (*ibid.*). A recent survey of Caithness in the sagas, undertaken by Cowan (1982), illustrates the importance of places like Freswick, Duncansby, Huna, Thurso, Stroma and Ham.

The archaeological evidence for Viking and Norse activity in Caithness comes in three main forms: settlements, graves and artefacts. Again, Batey has extensively reviewed these on a number of occasions (Batey 1987a; 1989; 1991a; 1991b;). The most revealing evidence comes from the graves. The earliest Viking grave from Caithness was found in 1786, in the top of a broch mound in Castletown (Wilson 1863, 265–6; Anderson 1874, 550; RCAHMS 1911, 87 no. 320). This grave contained a pair of tenth-century oval tortoise brooches, a lignite arm ring and a bone bodkin. In the early 1840s, another pair of tortoise brooches was found in a cist at the top of a gravel mound in Longhills (Westerseat). Although it is impossible to prove a direct link, the grave was located near the Kettleburn broch (Anderson 1874, 551–2).

REAY

The finest collection of Viking graves from the county was recovered at Reay on the northern coast. Coastal erosion has revealed a number of graves and various stray finds. Although it is difficult to prove, the site may be a cemetery (Curle, J. 1914; Grieg 1940; Edwards 1929; Graham-Campbell & Batey 1998, 125).

On the 3 October 1912 the *Glasgow Herald* reported the recovery of a buckle, taken to be a horse bridle, in close proximity to a skeleton. This was assumed to be a Viking burial (Batey 1987a, 139; 1987b, 35; 1993, 152). The possibility of a Viking connection at Reay was strengthened in September 1913: another burial was discovered when the wind blew aside the loose sand at Reay Links, exposing a human skull 4 feet below the surface. No cist was discovered and the few recovered bones suggest the body was laid in the sand, possibly in a doubled-up position (Curle, J. 1914, 295). One foot below the skull and situated upon the body were a pair of oval tortoise brooches, placed face-to-face. Near them lay remains of an iron bridle-bit, a bronze pin and buckle, and a stone spindle whorl. Found in the vicinity were an iron buckle and a small 'cross' which are generally accepted to be part of the grave. Portions of horse remains were found in the vicinity later. But there was more to come.

In a previous section we saw that Arthur Edwards excavated at Ackergill Pictish cemetery. In the introduction to his publication he noted that:

> In Caithness, when one considers that the county was held by the Vikings for a period of over five hundred years, it certainly does seem extraordinary that only three graves have been recorded – those at Castletown, Longhills, and Reay – which can be identified as having belonged to this period of occupation. I believe that not only have many Viking graves been unearthed without being recognised, but that there are probably others still to be brought to light (Edwards 1926, 160).

How ironic that the very year he published those words (1926), and when he was working in Caithness, he was to receive a telegram from his boss. In the third week of August, his director instructed him to proceed to Reay to record the discovery of another Viking grave which had been found by Robert MacKay and John Carmichael. They had been drawn to the area after seeing portions of leg bones protruding from the sand. The grave was 6 feet below the surface. By the time Edwards arrived, the grave had already been opened and the relics found carefully preserved by Rev. Mr Carmichael, minister of the parish.

Edwards set to work on recording the remains. He notes that the male skeleton was lying fully extended on a paved surface, his head raised on a flat stone. At the bottom of the grave was a stratum of dark-coloured sand mixed with pieces of slag and burnt iron. Edwards notes that the other relics consisted of: an iron axe; a shield boss; a knife;

a sickle; a cleat-shaped object; a buckle; and a rivet. A bronze pin was also found. Objects other than metal were a whetstone and two fragments of flint.

During his work on the grave, Edwards (1927, 203) 'saw numerous traces of what must either be graves or other regularly constructed works in stone'. This caused him to return to the area in 1928. He excavated a number of small mounds and other likely grave sites, but no new Viking graves were found. Instead, he recovered a series of circular structures, that were possibly parts of constructions, although he did not excavate any. However, he did excavate three cists, which had no associated relics. He also found a crushed pot, two hammerstones, a flint scraper and a bronze strap-end (Edwards 1929, 138–9). The strap-end probably dates to around the eighth or ninth century.

OTHER GRAVES?

Unsurprisingly, we have to turn to the work of Colleen again for insight into other possible Viking graves, and indeed settlements. At Dunnet, three mounds shaped like inverted boats were suggested by Anderson to be Norse ship burials (Batey 1987b, 39). In 1935, there were further tantalising indications of the presence of a Viking boat burial at Huna. A cairn in Halkirk was examined in 1850 and revealed several stone cists and human remains. These were associated with bronze rings and iron spearheads, but there is no proof that the cairn is Norse in date. At Watten an iron spearhead was found in or near a cist, but it is unclear what date the spearhead is. Many human bones have been found at Murkle and this may be a Late Norse nunnery. At Wester broch, Birkle Hills, Anderson noted four long cists deposited in the mound, which may mimic the Castlehill grave. The recent recovery of brooches from Thurso and Harrow may also suggest the presence of graves in the area.

11. VIKING SETTLEMENTS AND MIDDENS

Serendipity often plays a significant role in the recovery of archaeological sites. This can range from a chance find whilst walking the dog through to freak storms. Skara Brae, arguably one of the most famous European archaeological sites, is a good case in point of the latter phenomenon. Indeed, the discovery of sites through storms and erosion has been, and still is today, one of the characteristics of northern mainland archaeology. In 2004 the Caithness Archaeological Trust (CAT) came second in the British Archaeology Silver Trowel Award for the greatest initiative shown in an archaeological project. First place went to Scottish Coastal Archaeology and the Problem of Erosion (SCAPE), which is managed by Tom Dawson. Established in 2001, SCAPE aims to research, conserve and promote the archaeology of Scotland's coast. In particular, they are especially interested in remains that are threatened by coastal erosion, and run the important 'Shorewatch' programme. Through this innovative programme, members of local communities are encouraged to, and assisted in, becoming involved in the locating, recording and monitoring of sites on Scotland's coast.

We have seen that, largely because of the historical texts and place names, and the recovery of graves during the late nineteenth and early twentieth centuries, a strong Viking presence in Caithness could be implied. Paradoxically, during this time there was no understanding of where the Vikings and their subsequent generations lived. For example, the 1911 RCAHMS *Inventory* failed to report any structural remains that were indicative of their presence. However, owing to acts of God – that is, storms and coastal erosion – this picture was about to change. Our knowledge of Viking/Late Norse settlement in Caithness is still very small, but what we do have was, at one time, quite literally falling into the sea.

Freswick

> Yearly these banks are eroded and driven farther back by the tempestuous winds
> (Curle 1939, 72).

In an age when our landscape appears to be increasingly affected by fluctuations in weather, the key is how we react to the circumstances. We cannot, quite literally, hold back the tide. Violent storms that scrape the archaeology out of the earth are one thing.

Noticing and interrogating the uncovered remains is another. For this to happen we have to rely on people recognising and reporting the archaeology.

In the National Museums Scotland Archaeology department there is a series of catalogues that record all objects owned by the museum. As with many museum collections, the objects are recovered in a variety of ways, but they are often revealed when the soil has been eroded, and are subsequently discovered by people walking their dogs. The NMS catalogues are littered with stray finds from Freswick Sands, many of which were recovered and donated by local man, Simon Bremner. The material has a wide date range, although a lot of the objects date to the Late Norse period (i.e. after the initial Viking incursions). This association is hardly surprising – from around the 11th century the name of Freswick flits across the pages of the sagas (see Curle 1939, 71–2).

We have already had cause to celebrate the contribution of A. O. Curle to the county's archaeology through his survey and excavations, but it was also his diligence that uncovered the first definitive evidence for Norse settlement to be found both in the county and in mainland Scotland. Curle was spurred on by the place-name evidence, the historical references and, more particularly, the grass-tempered pottery, which is so similar to that uncovered at the Viking settlement at Jarlshof, Shetland, and which has been from time to time sent into the National Museum. He set to work in June 1937 and carried on for a further period of six weeks in the summer of 1938. Personal associations were, again, central to Curle's work. It was Arthur Edwards, by now the director of the National Museum of Antiquities, who drew Curle's attention to the site. Work on the ground relied heavily on local individuals. Simon Bremner again was a key contributor, supervising the locals who excavated the site with 'such zeal and interest beyond the mere terms of their employment as to deserve special recognition' (Curle 1939, 109). The local librarian even lent Curle a tent.

Three years after Curle stopped his excavations, Gordon Childe – one of the leading figures in European prehistory – returned to Freswick to dig, as in the title of his 1943 publication, 'Another late Viking House at Freswick' (Childe 1943). Erosion again was a key factor: the great storms of 1940 blew the sand from the tops of the walls of another complex suite of structures, to the north-east of Curle's excavations. Again, Simon Bremner was of great importance. He informed the inspector of ancient monuments that the newly exposed complex was endangered. As the sand was needed for government work, and because the structures could not be preserved, Childe excavated them before their removal. His work, which he himself termed a 'rescue dig' was funded by the Society of Antiquaries of Scotland. Simon Bremner again offered his services, as did Peter Kennedy, a scholar at Wick High School.

The works of Curle and Childe have been reviewed, assessed and discussed on numerous occasions by Colleen and this need not be repeated in detail here. However, it is pertinent to note that Curle recorded seven structures, published as Groups A, B and C, which may date to different periods (Fig 11.1). Group A formed the largest group and consisted of four buildings and a possible boat noust. Groups B and C were represented by single buildings. Childe also uncovered a particularly complex series of structures and distinguished three phases of activity. Numerous relics were recovered,

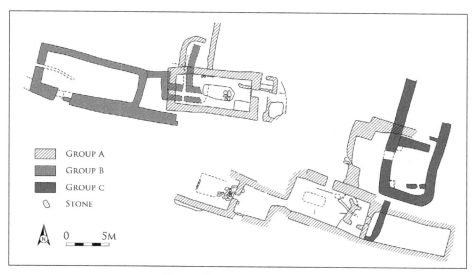

Fig 11.1 Viking settlement, Freswick

the majority of which were indicative of occupation in the Late Norse period. That said, work by Colleen and her associates suggests that there had been settlement and/ or activity in the Viking period (Morris, Batey & Rackham 1995, 271).

In the intervening years, the unsympathetic sea and winds continued to batter the north-east bay. Simon Bremner continued to recover and donate objects to the National Museum. As well as the structures and artefacts that fell out of the scars, the discovery of middens also continued. Although Curle and Childe were no doubt aware of these rich middens, like many enthusiasts of their day, they were focussed on the structural and artefactual record. In 1978, Colleen Batey and Christopher Morris returned to Freswick; they concentrated on the eroding coastal margins and, to a lesser extent, on one of the buildings (VI) first excavated by Curle. In particular, they focussed on the vast midden dumps in the area, in the hope of elucidating a series of research questions that were specifically linked to the environment and the economy (Batey 1987b; Morris, Batey & Rackham 1995).

One of the most interesting elements in the faunal assemblage is the fish bone, which suggests evidence of fishing on a large scale, which was possibly even commercial. This is of crucial significance owing to the rarity of this type of site on the western side of the North Sea and because of the implications for trading networks in northern Scotland. At Freswick, there were probably significant surpluses of small saithe, and large cod and ling, which could have underpinned an exchange network, at least within the Caithness hinterland. Perhaps at Freswick, as Morris Batey & Rackham (1995, 273) suggest, we should visualise a professional fishers' settlement with small-scale fish drying facilities, with the fish destined for local markets, and locals' bellies.

ROBERTSHAVEN

The value of systematic surveys is shown well by the suggestion of more Viking remains within the county. One of the sites discovered in the last quarter of a century is Robertshaven, on the north coast, to the east of John O'Groats (Ness of Duncansby). The site appears to be very similar to Freswick, on a number of levels. It is located in a sheltered bay and there are extensive middens with artefactual and ecofactual remains, including fish. There are also hints of structures. In 1992, a sampling project began, again with a focus on investigating the environmental and economic remains. Indeed, the site was excavated to produce a closely dated, well-preserved and adequately recovered fish-bone assemblage (Barrett 1997).

DUNNET

In 1992, Lesley Myatt submitted an entry to *Discovery and Excavation in Scotland*. It related to a midden site that contained seashells, fragments of animal, and fish bones that had been exposed owing to erosion of a dune area at Marymass Green, Dunnet. There was also evidence of stone walling. As part of Highland Archaeology Week 1995, Tony Pollard and the local community decided to undertake a small-scale evaluation excavation. The primary aim was to assess the date, function and extent of the archaeological features that were being revealed as the sand dune was eroded. These were cut back, cleaned and the archaeological remains recorded. Examination of the section face suggested that the exposed archaeological deposits ran back into the body of the dune, possibly for some considerable distance. In order to verify this, a series of small trenches were excavated on the summit of the dune and around its edges. Archaeological features and buried land surfaces were detected in a number of these trenches, indicating the presence of archaeological deposits beneath much of the area now occupied by the remnant dune. Archaeological deposits within the trial trenches were subject to the minimum degree of excavation necessary to achieve the aims of the evaluation (Pollard 1999, 149). The excavations uncovered shell middens, drystone walls, buried land surfaces and artefacts, including a Viking comb. The artefacts suggest that the site might have witnessed human activity over some considerable time, possibly extending from the pre-Viking to Late Norse periods (*ibid*. 154).

Although it has long been thought that there were only two *bus* (Old Norse: chieftain's farm) in Caithness – one at Freswick and the other at Duncansby –the stray finds and the limited excavations at Dunnet clearly show that we should expect to find other Viking sites, probably on the north coast. At Dunnet, the recovery of middens, the location on a sandy beach and the Viking comb suggest that this bay is ripe for further research. Indeed, since the excavation took place, pottery has been recovered from rabbit holes in other grass-covered dunes in fields across the road from Pollard's site. Areas of wall foundations and paving have also been noted. Indeed, Pollard (*ibid*. 156) was keen to stress that the archaeological significance of the area is not limited to the immediate vicinity of his excavated trenches. The entire area currently occupied by the sand dunes in Dunnet Bay is potentially crucial for our understandings of Viking/

Late Norse activity in Caithness. Unsurprisingly, we are not the first to think so: John Nicolson did too, when he painted the area under the banner of 'Gate of the Viking Age' (Fig. 11.2).

Although the Viking remains at Dunnet are undoubtedly important for us, the area is as noteworthy for being the home of Paul Humphreys, one of the best archaeologists in the county. It was he who found the pottery in and around Dunnet, as well as the Viking comb. After working with him on a number of occasions, this is of little surprise. His commitment, dedication and knowledge are second to none.

Another strong advocate for developing the county's heritage is Muriel Murray, chairwoman of Castletown Heritage Society, which is one of the best and most active heritage societies in Scotland.

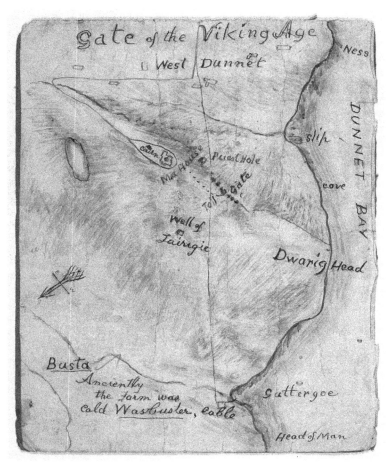

Fig 11.2 Nicolson's sketch of the 'Gate of the Viking Age', Dunnet (copyright RCAHMS)

12. WELLS

During the 2006 excavations in and around Keiss, one group of individuals were crucial to our work: local teachers and schoolchildren. We have already mentioned Rhona MacPherson of Keiss but other teachers from across the county came to visit, along with their children.

WHITEGATE WELL

In 2006, we began excavations of the roundhouse at Whitegate. One particular feature interested the children – a hole in the ground that it seemed had once been covered by a lintel. As far as we can tell from photographs and Anderson's (1901) brief report, Tress Barry did not excavate the feature. Discussions with local people told us that the hole periodically filled with water. As with so much fieldwork, we did not have time to fully excavate the hole's interior during 2006. We left it as a tantalising feature – could it be a grave, perhaps even Viking?

When we returned to Whitegate a year later we had the pleasure again of being joined by Rhona and other members of the Keiss community. Most archaeologists, young and old, want to find something exciting and so the team returned religiously every day for a fortnight in the hope that we would reopen the hole discovered the previous year. But we have already seen that our attentions were preoccupied by other events – in particular the bone deposit in the walls – and our attempts to understand other aspects of the site, specifically the area outside the roundhouse. It was of little surprise that the young army were frustrated – why are we digging a 2-metre-high rubble wall, when we could be digging the mysterious black hole in the interior?

Eventually our co-director, Jon Henderson, insisted we open up the 2006 trench, and with enormous enthusiasm and excitement, Rhona and her helpers began work on the mysterious hole in the ground. Once the full extent of the feature was exposed, a boat-shaped outline appeared. At first we thought it might be a grave after all, but, although we racked our brains for comparable Viking boat burials, this seemed unlikely. And the locals (surprise, surprise) were right: the feature consistently filled with water. Donning her yellow hard hat, Rhona then got into the hole and with the aid of others began to dig down. A step was discovered.

And then another.

And then another.

More mud, water and stone was removed until finally, a week later, Rhona realised that she had revealed a boat-shaped stepped structure, 2 metres deep. This truly remarkable site (Fig. 12.1) sent us scurrying to our books and contacts. Although we knew of similar, admittedly larger and grander, examples in Orkney, what were the Caithness comparanda? Given the number of previous broch excavations in the county, other individuals must surely have uncovered similar features. It did not take long to find an answer, and we returned again to Anderson and Rhind.

KETTLEBURN, KEISS AND OTHERS

During investigation of Kettleburn broch, Rhind discovered a series of, presumably secondary, walls and structures. One of these components overlay 'a regularly built well about nine feet deep, roofed over, so as to afford a basis for that part of the wall that passed over it, and accessible by steps' (Rhind 1853, 215). He noted that although not unique,

Fig 12.1 The well at Whitegate under excavation

such features were unusual, particularly examples of the quality he recovered. A few decades later, when Joseph Anderson was writing his summary of various excavations of five brochs in Caithness, he noted that when the farmer trenched the centre of the Ha' of Bowermadden broch he found a 'well with twelve or fourteen steps leading down to it' (1890a, 143).

Tress Barry and Nicolson also found similar features inside their broch interiors. In the interior of Keiss Road broch was a 5.5-feet-deep 'underground chamber with steps down into it, covered with slabs' (Anderson 1901, 135-136). The nearby Keiss Harbour broch also had a well, 6 feet deep, with four steps leading down to it. At the Hill of Works a well 2 feet deep, which was reached by a series of stairs, was found in front of the entrance to the intramural stairs. Most of these nineteenth-century features are only described by the written word. There are few schematic plans and it is difficult to be sure of the nature of many of these subterranean features. There is also little indication of their date.

We are on surer ground with the well feature at Crosskirk, which was excavated in the 1960s. The quadrilateral well was 7 feet deep, most of which (almost six and a half feet) had been cut into solid rock. Three rough steps descended into the cavity. The excavator, Horace Fairhurst, believed that the well was one of the earliest features in the interior of the broch (1984, 55–8); this suggests that he believed that the well dated to the construction and/or initial use of the broch. But it could have been earlier. The well was found hidden under the primary paving of the broch and almost immediately in front of the door to the stairs, in a position where it was difficult to see how it could have been a part of the original furnishings of the building. Not only was its situation inconvenient for users of the stairs but it had also been flagged over and sealed with clay (see Fairhurst 1984, 57–8).

However, our research also revealed similar structures outside roundhouses. Outside the broch entrance at Hillhead, six steps led down into a well that was 8 feet deep. The broch of Ness was cut off from the mainland by a cross-promontory wall and ditch; beside the entrance was another well, 9.5 feet deep, with 12 steps. It may be important that these examples were outside the roundhouse, and associated with entrances. Indeed, the Ness example is outside the promontory wall, the physical entity that is supposed to seal off and distance the community from the outside. One would assume that if the features provided a water supply, such a valuable commodity would be kept inside the living area.

There are other examples of well-like features that have been found in Caithness. There is an antiquarian reference to a possible broch at Scorriclet in Watten. Two 'underground rooms' and a well were supposed to have been discovered years ago. At Oust, near Thurso, a rock-cut well – 3.43 metres in depth – was recorded, which had 14 rock-cut steps and was roofed with converging slabs. This feature may be associated with a broch but no traces of the roundhouse survive today. It will, of course, be of little surprise to you, to hear that Paul Humphreys has been instrumental in the excavation and recording of a similar structure in recent times. We are grateful to Paul for the information, from which the following account is taken. In 1999, George Watson of the Caithness Field Club was notified of what appeared to be walling and a 'well' at Hoy Pool Farm, Halkirk. The area is best known for being the site of a broch. George immediately informed The Highland Council Archaeology Unit who believed the visible remains were significant enough to be recorded. Together with Janet Hooper (Project Officer with the Archaeology Unit), Barbara Hiddleston, George Watson and Paul set to work. A stone-lined polygonal chamber with corbelling towards the top was discovered (Feature C).

So what are these peculiar features and what date are they?

MacKie (2007, 413) suggests that it is possible – even likely – that the Crosskirk well was on the site when the broch was built and is connected with Late Bronze Age occupation. The possible Bronze Age sherd found inside the well may support this view. Similar, and better known, well features are known from Orkney, for example Gurness (Hedges 1987). Again, dating these feature is difficult, but it is likely that they date to the original construction and use of the broch, if not before. Indeed, as many were dug into the natural bedrock and boulder clay it seems logical that most, if not all, of this work would have been completed before the broch was built.

As regards function, in the past it has been assumed that these wells or cisterns were either for getting water or storing it. There are numerous problems with this scenario. First, the elaborate nature of the features suggests that their use went far beyond the functional. For example, steps are unnecessary in a well: lowering a bucket on a rope would do nicely. The extraordinary degree of elaboration seen on many sites, for what must have been a very inadequate water supply, must be accounted for (Armit 2003). Indeed, it is arguable if they were for water supply at all. Further, excavated examples across Caithness and Orkney were dry, with no evidence for dampness or water to suggest a spring; although, of course, it is possible that the level of the water table has changed over the intervening 2,000 years. Indeed, being so close to the sea must have meant that salt water infiltrated the water and contaminated the supply (Harding 2004, 127). This is not to dispute that there were was a need for water and/or wells on Atlantic Scottish sites; some sites in Caithness have reference to wells or pits with no mention of steps leading down into them, such as Skirza (Anderson 1901, 145), Harpsdale and Dunbeath (Anderson 1890a, 144–5). We simply wish to highlight that these elaborate stepped examples probably had a deeper meaning than the purely functional and/or domestic. This is evidenced at Midhowe, where a spring within the broch supplies water to a tank at ground level, whereas access to the subterranean is gained by an underground structure, which also lies within the central area of the broch. The recent recovery of an extremely elaborate example from Mine Howe also shows the non-domestic purpose of these features. Discussing the feature, Card & Downes (2003, 17) state:

> The subterranean nature of these structures seems to have been of overriding importance, aside of whether they held water that could be artificially or naturally supplied. At Mine Howe an elaborate and large example of this type of structure has been discovered, surrounded by a huge ditch but *not* situated within or underneath a broch – surely a clear indication of the significance and ritual sanctity of these structures. The Mine Howe site causes us to re-evaluate existing data on brochs, and makes the relationship between brochs and associated underground structures a focus for future research.

We can do little but agree.

13. ARTEFACTS

During the 1880s, Mr Christie was searching for something in his Edinburgh flat. Scrabbling through some loose papers in the bottom of a trunk he came upon, accidentally, a silver object that had been given to him two decades previously. He found the object curious and after consultation with a friend who knew something of silversmiths' work he took it to the local jewellers, Messrs William Marshall & Co. on Princes Street, the main thoroughfare of the Scottish capital. One of the employees, Mr John Marshall, was intrigued by the find and contacted our old friend Joseph Anderson of the National Museum of Antiquities, in Edinburgh. When the two met, Marshall was armed with a broken piece of jewellery and he kindly offered his services in securing it for the National Museum of Antiquities, should Anderson desire such an acquisition. Anderson bit his hand off.

THE ACHAVROLE BROOCH

Today, if you were to open any account of Early Christian Art in Britain and Ireland there are a few key objects that would recur in all studies including the Tara brooch, the Ardagh chalices and Derrynaflan hoard. In Scotland, the Monymusk reliquary and the Hunterston brooch would dominate any account. But hidden within many accounts would be the poorly studied fragmentary object called the 'Achavrole' or 'Dunbeath' brooch (Fig. 13.1). This was the object in Marshall's overcoat pocket.

Marshall produced one half of a silver penannular brooch, its upper surface was adorned with plates of thin gold inserted in panels. The panels are beautifully ornamented with twisted animals and S-shaped scrolls, formed from gold filigree and twisted gold wire, which are soldered onto the surface. Circular and rectangular panels house amber settings. This is one of the key objects in Scotland's Early Historic repertoire.

The brooch had been found many years before, in 1860, and after consultation with Christie, Anderson wrote to the original finder, William Sutherland. Anderson learnt that the fragment brought to him by Marshall was all that was – and is now – known to exist of the original item, but Mr Sutherland also provided some other valuable information as to the context and nature of the find.

He found the brooch in a drain that he was digging for his house. He intimated that the brooch may have been wrapped in leather or cloth as he 'got an intimation of this

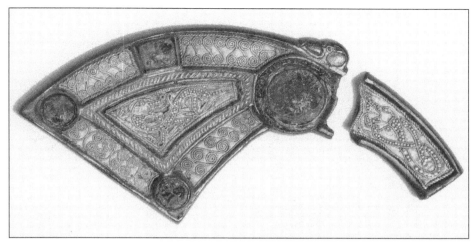

Fig 13.1 The magnificent brooch from Dunbeath (copyright National Museums Scotland)

about it'. During his operations his pick disfigured the whole apparatus out of its form and as soon as the object was touched all of the stone settings fell out of their sockets. The question must be asked, therefore, who put the surviving settings back? He also noted that 'there was something similar to a Roman Catholic cross in the middle of this old brooch, and a great deal of other articles attached to it … there was a cross coming through the centre of it' (quoted in Anderson 1880, 448–9). Did this suggest that the brooch was not penannular but, perhaps, more akin to the annular brooches with arguably Christian iconography, perhaps even comparable to the iconic Hunterston brooch?

Anderson was dismayed. Although the fragment of the brooch was significant, the 'lost' portions were even more so. Anderson noted that, 'it is on this account the more to be regretted that the larger portion of the Dunbeath brooch should have perished through simple want of care, and ignorance of its value' (*ibid.* 448). Mr Sutherland's letter would not have helped. He wrote:

> I have to inform you that I have got none of this old brooch; or I don't know of any one in this place that has got any of this old stuff you speak about. The time is so long since that everything about it is out of sight and mind here.

Anderson noted that such a reply was characteristic, presumably in reference to some of his day-to-day workings as a custodian of the nation's treasures. Fast-forward a hundred and thirty years.

No one likes to do bad things. No speeding, no drink driving, no talking in church or on your phone in the car. But for one to do bad things, one has to know what a bad thing is. And in Scotland there is a well-founded, correct process, but one that, in our experience, many people have not heard of. This is not an excuse for ignoring the process.

The Treasure Trove system safeguards portable antiquities of archaeological, historical and cultural significance found in Scotland. Operation of the Treasure

Trove system in relation to portable antiquities found in Scotland, and decisions on the allocation of finds to museums and the level of any ex gratia payment, lie with the Queen's and Lord Treasurer's Remembrancer (QLTR). The QLTR is advised by the Scottish Archaeological Finds Allocation Panel and supported by the Treasure Trove Unit (TTU) and the QLTR Office.

In a nutshell found items from anywhere in Scotland (on land, in buildings, from inland waters, from within harbours, and from the coast and other tidal waterways down to mean low tidal water level) which are not otherwise owned and for which there is not a demonstrable heir (bona vacantia) are the property of the Crown at Scots common law. Portable antiquities form a subset of bona vacantia. Found portable antiquities must be reported to the Crown by the finder through the Treasure Trove Unit or an appropriate intermediary (e.g. a museum). Misappropriation of found portable antiquities is the crime of theft and dishonest dealing in such items is the crime of reset, or receiving stolen property. Failure to report the finding of portable antiquities or the removal of found portable antiquities from Scotland (including to elsewhere in the United Kingdom) may provide evidence of misappropriation. Cases of apparent dishonesty will be reported to the Procurator Fiscal or Police for investigation and consideration of criminal proceedings. Offences are punishable by a fine or a term of imprisonment or both.

Non-reported portable antiquities cannot be owned by anyone else if the Crown has not been given the opportunity, by reporting, of exercising its right of ownership. There is no time limit with respect to non-reporting of items which thus remain the property of the Crown in perpetuity. Finders have no ownership rights to found objects which have not been reported to the Crown. Landowners have no property rights to portable antiquities, nor do sponsors of organised archaeological fieldwork have any claim to any finds made on their projects. Finders must ensure they have any appropriate permission to search land for portable antiquities.

Many chance finds are made with the aid of a metal detector. It is a criminal offence (under section 42 of the Ancient Monuments and Archaeological Areas Act 1979) to use a metal detector on a scheduled monument or a monument in the ownership or guardianship of Scottish Ministers, or of a Local Authority, without prior written permission from.

Bronze Age metals

There is a significant, yet inadequately studied, collection of metal objects from Caithness that gives a useful insight into the metal objects that were in circulation around 3,000 years ago. To the authors' knowledge there have been at least twenty objects discovered that span the Early to Late Bronze Age, although not all of them survive. Most of them are currently in the National Museums Scotland. The bronze corpus comprises a range of objects including various types of axe, spearheads and swords. The Hillhead hoard, which comprises two gold penannular armlets contained in a stone bowl, is perhaps the most impressive part of the metal corpus. Although each class has a small number of specimens, and distribution maps can be misleading, the object range is consistent with the wider Scottish suite (see Coles 1960; 1964; 1969 for a useful summary).

Like the Achavrole brooch, almost all of the bronze objects from the county were found during the late nineteenth or early twentieth centuries and records of many of the find spots are vague to say the least. Often, we know little more than the objects were found somewhere in the county or within particular parish boundaries. Other records, for example the axes from Broubster or Keiss and the sword from Mey, refer only to the village or area in which they were found. But can we tease out further information? What do the find spots of the other objects tell us?

Cnocan Dubh spearhead was found in a landscape now characterised by open peatland and heathery hills (Close-Brooks 1975, 194). The find spot, about one hundred metres above sea level, has no other archaeological monuments in the vicinity. Similarly, the spearhead from Rowens Hill, which may be Bronze Age, was recovered from an equally remote, peaty area with no archaeological monuments nearby. The Blingery Moor chisel was also recovered from peatland barren of monuments. Conversely, other finds were recovered in landscapes peppered with Neolithic or Bronze Age monuments. Two objects from Yarrows and Lower Howe appear to be associated with burial cairns: the Yarrows knife was found in a cist. The Forse sword was deposited in an estate that was, as we have seen, awash with archaeological monuments, including standing stones, cairns and hut circles. The Lower Dounreay axe was deposited within a landscape of Neolithic and Bronze Age monuments, including numerous chambered cairns and stone rows. The landscape is also the highest natural mound in the area. A similar connection between monuments and prominent landscape features relates to the socketed axe from Warth Hill, found downslope of the cist cairn excavated by Anderson. Warth Hill is the highest, most visible landmass in the north-east of the county; from there you have clear views to the Orkneys.

Aside from noting their existence what more do these objects tell us? Recent studies have illustrated how careful analysis of Bronze Age metalwork can provide insight into the production, social use and deposition of metal objects. Central to many discussions has been a colleague and friend of ours, Trevor Cowie, who is senior curator in the archaeology department of the National Museums Scotland. Without question, Trevor is one of Europe's leading experts, if not *the* leading expert, on the Bronze Age. What Trevor doesn't know about the Bronze Age, particularly in Scotland, isn't worth knowing. In recent articles, Trevor and others have emphasised how a significant proportion of Bronze Age metalwork survives for us to study precisely because it was deliberately taken out of circulation: the objects were placed in the ground, probably in places of special significance. The locations of these 'special places' can be numerous. Some were natural places, such as mountains, hilltops, caves, rivers, lochs and coastlines (see also Bradley, 2000 for a good summary). Natural geological formations may also have had significance for the deposition of metalwork. Special places also involved the built environment: that is, monuments constructed by people. Objects could be deposited in or near a monument that was either contemporary or from an earlier period.

These wider British studies may have resonance with the Caithness record. A fair proportion of the Caithness repertoire was found within the natural environment, particularly in remote areas now covered in peat, and apparently devoid of archaeological monuments. Although monuments may lie undetected underneath the peat, this surely cannot be true in all cases. There are enough peatlands in the county with recognisable monuments. It is, therefore, highly likely that some bronze objects were deposited in remote, barren landscapes. This pattern could suggest some form of connection between the deposition of metalwork and liminal locations where notions of wilderness, and possibly water, were significant. Conversely, these metal deposits may have marked symbolic boundaries, perhaps demarcating neighbouring communities or separating the domestic landscape from the wild or other worlds. With this is mind it is noteworthy that the Cnocan Dubh spearhead was found very close to the modern day Caithness–Sutherland border. The use of natural places as arenas for deposition may also be illustrated by the axes from Lower Dounreay and Warth Hill. As noted, these two finds were deposited within some of the most prominent natural mounds in the north-east and north-west of the county. This use of natural, prominent mounds for the deposition of metalwork might have been mimicked in the construction of man-made mounds, such as cairns.

But what of the deposition of metalwork in areas peppered with Neolithic or Bronze Age monuments? We have seen throughout this book that particular areas and landscapes were accorded significance in the past. As in today's world, people in prehistory engaged with their history to make meaningful statements. This surely explains the occurrence of various forms of Bronze Age activity on or near, for example, Neolithic chambered cairns. And with this in mind we must remember the numerous Bronze Age burials were positioned on, or near, Neolithic chambered tombs. Bradley (2002, 34) has called this the 'origin myth', through which people in the past used monuments to remember, and to create some sense of their own past. This may explain why later inhabitants kept on returning to the area first marked by the Neolithic.

This, of course, presumes that the metal objects were deposited in the Bronze Age. Is this true for all of the finds? Although noting that the penannular bracelets from Hillhead were similar to other examples from the Late Bronze Age, Curle (1913, 435) did note that the stone bowl bears a general resemblance in character and finish to similar objects found in Iron Age brochs. The dating of stone objects is notoriously difficult and the vessel could equally be of any date. Hillhead broch sits less than a mile from where the bowl and bracelets were found. Similarly, according to the National Museums Scotland continuation catalogue, the axe from Keiss was found near Keiss broch, although it is impossible to be sure which of the three brochs the comment is referring to. This may suggest that Bronze Age objects were curated: precious, symbolic items that were integral to socio-political trajectories in the Iron Age.

14. YET MORE CIRCLES AND MOUNDS ... AND JELLY BABIES

By now, it should be clear that our understanding of Caithness' archaeology is biased. First, and for whatever reason, we can really only approach the study of the first 6,000 years of human activity in the county through the burial record: we have yet to discover the houses and settlements. Second, although surveys since the nineteenth century have revealed the wealth and breadth of the archaeological remains, we still have a tendency to concentrate on a limited range of sites: in particular chambered cairns and brochs. Although parts of this partiality are being addressed by recent work on stone rows and henges, there is still a significant body of data, especially settlements, that we need to start grappling with in future years if we are to begin to construct a more rounded view of Caithness' prehistory.

HUT CIRCLES

With the possible exception of brochs and/or Atlantic roundhouses, the largest body of archaeological evidence from the county comes in the form of hut circles. Convention tells us that there may be as many as 185 sites or clusters in the county. The majority are confined to the uplands of the south and west, where 'hut circle landscapes' are often preserved (Cowley 1999, 68–70, Fig. 2a). The recent LiDAR surveys of Baillie and Yarrows suggest that there are more hut circles peppered across these landscapes than previously thought (see www.aocarchaeology/Baillie). Although it has been argued that structures at Ackergill and Langwell are hut circles (e.g. Cree 1911), it is the authors' belief that, until 2012 when one of us (AH) and our colleagues Graeme Cavers and Charlotte Douglas excavated a small trench across a hut circle near Watenan, few, if any, hut circles had been excavated in the county. Although Cowley's (2005, 181–2) suggestion that the distribution of brochs in the lowlands of Caithness is in complete contrast to that of the hut circles, there are some areas of notable overlap, particularly in the areas around Yarrows, Forse and Dunbeath (Fig. 14.1; *ibid*. Fig. 53).

Although the dating of hut circles in Caithness is largely unknown, Cowley (2005, 181) has suggested that many could date to the second millennium BC and the first half of the first millennium BC. This may suggest that by the mid-first millennium BC and the beginning of the first millennium AD, hut-circle settlements were replaced by other

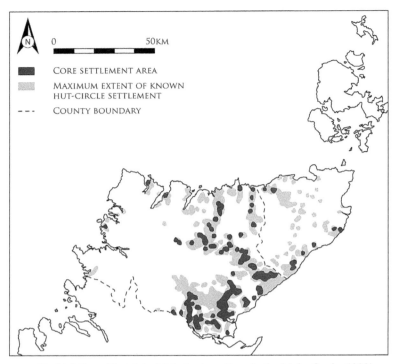

Fig 14.1 General hut circle distribution in northern Scotland (after Cowley 1999)

structures. However, we should be aware that the relatively limited dating available for other Scottish hut circles indicates that the type was a highly successful form which persisted for at least the last two millennia BC, and perhaps into the early centuries AD (Barber 1997; Carter 1993; Fairhurst & Taylor 1971: McCullagh & Tipping 1998). This latter suggestion is supported by our recent work on the Watenan hut circle.

As with other site characterisations, there are clear differences in size and structural features within the catch-all 'hut circle' definition, which perhaps reflects different chronologies, functions and status. An assessment of hut circles in Sutherland has identified recurrent patterns in the juxtaposition of houses and the remains of certain types of land use, which may suggest a zoning in settlement intensity: with core areas of potentially long-lived settlement being associated with developed field systems, and peripheral areas being related to more transient or perhaps seasonal activity (Cowley 1998; 1999, 69). It is also clear from the evidence that there may have been repeated stages of construction of some hut-circle types (Barber 1997; McCullagh & Tipping 1998) and that prehistoric settlement in many areas underwent cycles of expansion and contraction during the first and second millennia BC, and probably later. All of these areas – date, function, status, land-use setting, and so on – change through time, and, more importantly, the reasons for them, are central to our understanding of the Iron Age settlement pattern in Caithness prior to, and possibly during, the construction of more visible structures such as brochs. Understanding Caithness hut circles should be a key priority for any future project in the county.

CRANNOGS

Another key settlement type that may aid our understanding of the Caithness Iron Age is the crannog. Crannogs, man-made artificial islands used for habitation, pepper Scottish waterways. The major concentrations are in the south-west, west and central areas of Scotland, although there are examples from other areas. Although many islands were used and reused in later time periods, dating from Scottish sites suggests that crannogs were built and occupied throughout the latter half of the first millennium BC and into the mid- to late first millennium AD. The majority of radiocarbon dated crannogs are of later prehistoric date (Crone 2012).

The study of crannogs has gathered momentum since the 1980s, which is shown well by the recent work of the Scottish Wetland Project and the publications by, for example, Anne Crone, Jon Henderson, Alex Hale and Graeme Cavers. The foundations of Scottish crannog studies were, however, laid by Robert Munro (1882) in the second half of the nineteenth century. A few decades later, there was a desire to map the extent of known artificial islands across the Scottish landscape. In 1910, the British Association appointed a committee with a view to ascertaining further information on these artificial islands. With a grant of £10 to cover incidental expenses, the committee issued a circular, of which 450 copies were sent out, in the hope that locals would inform the committee of crannogs in their neighbourhood. The Rev. F. Odo Blundell acted as liaison and published the numerous replies in 1913.

The committee wrote to Mr Robert M'Clements, Schoolhouse, Keiss, who in turn communicated with our old friend John Nicolson, owing to his thorough acquaintance with the archaeology of the county. They suggested that six sites were artificial islands: Loch Toftingall, Loch Rangag, Loch Alterwall, Loch Watten, Loch of Stemster (Scarmclate) and Loch Calder. It is clear from the 1913 descriptions and a recent survey by Graeme Cavers that not all of these sites are crannogs in the true sense of the word. According to Cavers perhaps only two sites can confidently be identified as artificial islets – those in Loch Watten and Loch of Yarrows. Of those sites none have timber as a major structural component. This may suggest that lake settlements were built in a similar fashion to other contemporary settlements in the area, that is, from stone. We should bear in mind that on the shores of Loch Rangag is a broch, locally known as Greysteil Castle, which may have sat on an artificial island, approached by a causeway. Again, these sites may be worth a closer look in the future.

Finally, we should remember that many artificial islands were used well into the medieval and post-medieval periods. This is shown by the excavation of Loch Alterwall by another old friend, Sir Francis Tress Barry. In 1900, he revealed a square building with an accompanying staircase (Blundell 1913, 285), now argued to be a tower. The excavations revealed a suite of medieval finds.

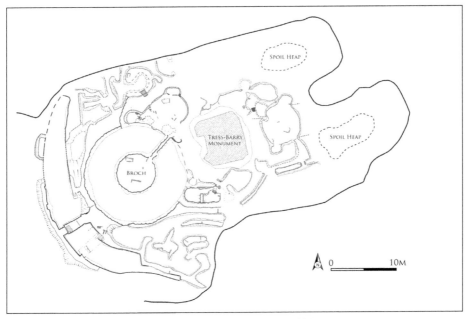

Fig 14.2 The cellular buildings at Nybster

CELLULAR BUILDINGS

Another part of the Iron Age settlement repertoire are cellular buildings, often called 'jelly-baby' houses. Since the 1970s, excavations in the Northern and Western Isles have consistently uncovered cellular structures of various types, with their form and geographical distribution leading them to be known variously as Pictish cellular, jelly-baby or ventral buildings. Although some (e.g. Buckquoy, Orkney; Bostadh, Lewis) are not directly associated with broch mounds, the majority have been uncovered during excavations of such sites. Until recent work at Nybster, no Caithness examples had been excavated in modern times, although surveys had clearly shown that cellular buildings existed in Caithness and that they were particularly focussed around broch mounds, for example at Keiss and Nybster (Fig. 14.2). Rightly or wrongly, there was a belief that many of the Caithness examples dated to the post-Roman period, continued to be functional into the Pictish period and perhaps went out of use when the Vikings invaded. Thus, there was a suggestion that during the second half of the first millennium AD, individuals and groups utilised various monument types (wags, cellular buildings, crannogs and reused roundhouses) in their everyday lives. This may still be true but recent work at Nybster has introduced a note of caution. In 2011, excavations showed that the cellular buildings were built and used between the first and third centuries AD, which suggested that there was at least some form of cellular-building tradition during the Roman Iron Age.

A few weeks digging of cellular buildings, hut circles and crannogs may begin to alter our long-held views on the Caithness Iron Age. Brochs are important, but continual focus on them may be masking a wider understanding of our past.

FORTS

In his 1972 discussion of the Iron Age of Caithness, Bramman (1972, 112) suggested that some hillforts and promontory forts may have been part of Early Iron Age defensive works and were, therefore, some of the earliest Iron Age structures in the county. The main structural work on these sites takes the form of massive embankments, which make the most of any natural features offered by the site. There are ten or eleven promontory sites in Caithness: Neck of Brough, Thurso; Holborn Head, Thurso; West Murkle, Thurso; St John's Point, Canisbay; Skirza Head broch, Canisbay; Broch of Ness, Canisbay; Sgarbach, Canisbay; Broch of Nybster, Wick; Gote o' Tram, Wick; and Bay of Girston, Wick (see Lamb 1980). Poll Gorm in Dunbeath may also be a promontory site.

The term 'promontory fort' conceals a variety of types. Many sites are defined as such because they are separated from the mainland by a bank/ditch of a very substantial nature. Some of the ditches have massive stone-revetted ramparts immediately inward of the ditch (e.g. Skirza Head and Ness). Others, for example Nybster, appear to be 'blockhouses', a structure that may have its origin within the general promontory-fort class (Lamb 1980, 6, 11). Good examples of hillforts can be found at Yarrows, Garrywhin, 'Cnoc na Ratha' (Shurrery) and 'Buaile Oscar' (Ben Friecidean) (Fig. 14.3). Although these could be part of the Iron Age repertoire, they could also be enclosures dating back to the Bronze Age or Neolithic periods and may not in fact be settlement forms at all, but ritual enclosures (Swanson 1992, 47). Again, if we are serious about understanding the Caithness Iron Age, we have to start exploring some of these fort sites more earnestly.

Fig 14.3 Ben Friecidean hillfort

15. SOME FINAL THOUGHTS

This book was never intended as a guidebook or a holistic overview of the county's riches. *Caithness Archaeology* has been our attempt to document the many different aspects of archaeology that we have experienced, encountered and researched during our time in the province so far. Central to the journey have been the end points – the destinations – and the book has been structured around archaeological sites and landscapes. However, in this book we have aspired to do more than produce a convenient overview of different settlement, burial and artefact types.

We wanted to accentuate other aspects of the archaeological record. In a very real sense the book is disjointed, with sections and sub-sections that bounce different ideas and concepts around. Although some parts are descriptive (you did read the section on wags?), other sections attempt to offer new interpretations of evidence that you may be familiar with. Other passages aim to navigate through the contrasting ways that different individuals in past, or indeed contemporary, times have interpreted the same archaeology. Where appropriate, we have highlighted some of the politics we have encountered with a particular focus on the preservation, protection, management and presentation of key archaeological sites and artefacts.

One of the main aims of the book has been to highlight the active individuals who have studied, promoted, enjoyed and lived with their heritage – and those who continue to do so. It is hopefully clear by now that the birth of Caithness – and arguably Scottish – prehistory was founded on the work of a handful of individuals working in the mid-nineteenth and early twentieth centuries. During this formative period, the county was a magnet for academic and intellectual endeavour that laid the foundations for many cultural, chronological and typological frameworks that are still debated today. But this archaeological work did not take place in a vacuum: it took place within a vibrant intellectual community comprising geologists, botanists, ornithologists, geographers and historians. This book is littered with references to the key individuals, such as Alexander H. Rhind, Joseph Anderson, Alexander Curle, Robert Shearer, Samuel Laing, Sir Francis Tress Barry, and John Nicolson. Their names have been mentioned time and time again in connection with a wide variety of monuments, periods, and geographical areas. We also hope we have pressed home the critical contribution today's communities play in our understanding and enjoyment of the county's archaeology. As you read this, Caithness is awash with individuals who know and appreciate their archaeology better than anyone else. They, and many of their ancestors, have lived and breathed their heritage.

If we have achieved anything in this book, we hope it has been to demonstrate that whilst we may pen the words that get published, it is the likes of John Nicolson, Simon Bremner, Alisdair Sutherland, Paul Humphreys, Rhona MacPherson, Muriel Murray, Sheila Gillen, and Nan and George Bethune who are the real champions of the county's stunning archaeology.

BIBLIOGRAPHY

Allen, J. R. & Anderson, J. 1903. *The Early Christian Monuments of Scotland*. Edinburgh.

Anderson, J. 1866a. Report on the ancient remains of Caithness, and results of explorations, *Memoirs of the Anthrop Soc of London*, 2, 226–56.

Anderson, J. 1866b. On the chambered cairns of Caithness, with results of recent explorations, *Proc Soc Antiq Scot*, 6 (1864–6), 442–51.

Anderson, J. 1868. On the horned cairns of Caithness: their structural arrangement, contents of chambers etc, *Proc Soc Antiq Scot*, 7 (1866–8), 480–512.

Anderson, J. 1872. Notice on the excavation of 'Kenny's Cairn', on the Hill of Bruan; Carn Righ, near Yarhouse; the Warth Hill Cairn, Duncansby; and several smaller sepulchral cairns in Caithness, *Proc Soc Antiq Scot*, 9 (1870–2), 292–6.

Anderson, J. 1874. Notes on the relics of the Viking period of the Northmen in Scotland, illustrated by specimens in the Museum, *Proc Soc Antiq Scot*, 10 (1872–4), 536–94.

Anderson, J 1880. 'Notice of a Fragment of a Silver Penannular Brooch, Ornamented with Gold Filigree Work and Amber Settings, found at Achavrole, Dunbeath, Caithness in 1860; and of Two Silver Brooches, the Property of Andrew Heiton, FSA Scot, Said to Have Been Found in the Neighbourhood of Perth', *Proc Soc Antiq Scot*, 14 (1879-1880), 445–452.

Anderson, J. 1881. *Scotland in Early Christian Times*. Edinburgh.

Anderson, J. 1883. *Scotland in Pagan Times: The Iron Age*. Edinburgh.

Anderson, J. 1886. *Scotland in Pagan Times: The Bronze & Stone Ages*. Edinburgh.

Anderson, J. 1890a. Notice of the excavation of the brochs of Yarhouse, Brounaben, Bowermadden, Old Stirkoke and Dunbeath in Caithness, with remarks on the period of the brochs; and an appendix, containing a collected list of the brochs of Scotland, and early notices of many of them, *Archaeologica Scotica*, 5 (1890), 131–98.

Anderson, J. 1890b. 'The Systematic Study of Scottish Archaeology', *Trans Glasgow Archaeol Soc*, NS 1 (1881–1890), 343–54.

Anderson, J. 1901. Notices of nine brochs along the Caithness coast from Keiss Bay to Skirza Head, excavated by Sir Francis Tress Barry, Bart, MP, of Keiss Castle, Caithness, *Proc Soc Antiq Scot*, 35 (1900–1), 112–48.

Anderson, J. 1908. The brochs of Caithness. Additions to the Antiquarian Museum, *The Scotsman*, Tuesday 21 July 1908.

Armit, I. 1990. Broch building in Northern Scotland: the context of innovation, *World Archaeol*, 21, 3 (1990), 435–45.

Armit, I. 1992. *The Later Prehistory of the Western Isles of Scotland*. Oxford (= Brit Archaeol Rep, 221).

Armit, I. 1996. *The Archaeology of Skye and the Western Isles*. Edinburgh.

Armit, I. 2003. *Towers in the North: The Brochs of Scotland*. Wiltshire.

Armit, I. 2006 *Anatomy of an Iron Age Roundhouse: The Cnip Wheelhouse Excavations, Lewis*, Edinburgh.

Armit, I. & Ginn, V. 2007. Beyond the grave: Human remains from domestic contexts in Iron Age Atlantic Scotland, *Proc Prehist Soc*, 73 (2007), 113–34.

Artelius, T. & Svanberg, F. (eds) 2005. *Dealing with the Dead: Archaeological Perspectives on Prehistoric Scandinavian Burial Ritual*. Riksantikvarieambetets forlag, Stockholm.

Ashmore, P. J. 1980. Low cairns, long cists and symbol stones, *Proc Soc Antiq Scot*, 110 (1978–80), 346–55.

Baines, A. 1999. Breaking the Circle: Archaeology and architecture in the Later Iron Age of northern Scotland, *Northern Archaeology*, 17/18 (1999), 77–85.

Baines, A. 2002. The inherited past of the broch: On antiquarian discourse and contemporary archaeology, *Scottish Archaeol. Jl*, 24:1, 1–20.

Baines, A., Brophy, K. & Pannett, A. 2003. Yarrows landscape project/Battle Moss stone rows, *Discovery & Excavation in Scotland*, ns 4, 94–5.

Ballin Smith, B. 1994. *Howe: Four Millennia of Orkney Prehistory*. Edinburgh (=Soc Antiq Scot Monogr Ser, 9).

Barber, J. 1997. *The archaeological investigation of a prehistoric landscape : excavations on Arran, 1987–81*. Edinburgh, Scottish Trust for Archaeological Research.

Barber, J., Cavers, G. & Heald, A. *forthcoming*. Memory in practice and the practice of memory in Caithness, NE Scotland, and in Sardinia', in Stoddart, S. & Malone, C. (eds), *Gardening Time: Reflections in Memory. Monuments and History in Scotland and Sardinia*. Oxford.

Barrett, J. H. 1992. Robert's Haven, *Discovery and Excavation in Scotland*: 40–1.

Barrett, J. H. 1997. Fish trade in Norse Orkney and Caithness: A zooarchaeological approach, *Antiquity*, 71, 616–38.

Barrett, J. H. 2003. Culture Contact in Viking Age Scotland, in Barrett, J. H. (ed), *Contact, Continuity and Collapse. The Norse Colonization of the North Atlantic*, 73–111. Belgium.

Batey, C. 1984. *Caithness Coastal Survey 1980–82: Dunnet Head to Ousdale*. Durham (=Durham Univ Occas Pap, 3).

Batey, C. 1987a. Viking and Late Norse Caithness: The archaeological evidence, in Knirk, J. (ed), *Proceedings of the Tenth Viking Congress, Larkollen, Norway 1985*, 131–48. Oslo. Universitetets Oldsaksamlings Skrifter Ny Rekke Nr 9.

Batey, C. 1987b. *Freswick Links, Caithness. A Reappraisal of the Late Norse Site in its Context*. Oxford (=Brit Archaeol Rep Brit Ser, 179, two vols).

Batey, C. 1989. Viking and Late Norse Caithness, in Omand, D. (ed) *The New Caithness Book*, 67–78. Wick.

Batey, C. 1991a. Picts and Vikings in Caithness and Sutherland: A resumé, in Karkov, C. & Farrell, R. (eds), *Studies in Insular Art and Archaeology*, 49–60. Miami, Ohio (=American Early Medieval Stud, 1).

Batey, C. 1991b. Archaeological aspects of Norse Settlement in Caithness, north Scotland, *Acta Archaeologica*, 61, 29–35.

Batey, C. E. 1993. The Viking and Late Norse graves of Caithness and Sutherland, in Batey, C. E., Jesch, J. & Morris, C. D. (eds), *The Viking Age in Caithness, Orkney and the North Atlantic*: 148–64. Edinburgh.

Beveridge, E. 1911. *North Uist: Its Archaeology and Topography, with Notes upon the Early History of the Hebrides*. Edinburgh.

Blackie, T. & Macaulay, C. 1998. *The Sculptured Stones of Caithness*. Angus.

Blundell, F. O. 1913. Further notes on the artificial islands in the Highland area, *Proc Soc Antiq Scot*, 47 (1912–13), 257–302.

Bradley, R. 2000. *An Archaeology of Natural Places*. London

Bradley, R. 2002. *The Past in Prehistoric Societies*. London and New York.

Bradley, R. 2005. *Ritual and Domestic Life in Prehistoric Europe*. Cambridge.

Bramman, J. I. 1972. The Early inhabitants, in Omand, D. (ed), *The Caithness Book*, 101–10. Inverness.

Bryce, T. H. 1905. Notes (1) on a human skeleton found in a cist with a Beaker urn at Acharole, West Watten, Caithness; and (2) on the cranial form associated with that type of ceramic. With an appendix on six skulls found with Beakers in the north-east counties, *Proc Soc Antiqs Scot*, 39 (1904–05), 418–38.

Burl, A. 1976. *The Stone Circles of the British Isles*. New Haven & London.

Burl, A. 1995. *A Guide to the Stone Circles of Britain, Ireland and Brittany*, Yale University Press (UK)

Cairnduna. 1916. Pulteney notes: the late Dr Joseph Anderson, *John O' Groats Journal*, Friday 6 October 1916, 4.

Campbell, E. 1991. Excavations of a wheelhouse and other Iron Age structures at Sollas, North Uist by R. J. C. Atkinson in 1957, *Proc Soc Antiq Scot*, 121 (1991), 117–73.

Card, N. & Downes, J. 2003. Mine Howe – the significance of space and place in the Iron Age, in Downes, J. & Ritchie, A. (eds), *Sea Change, Orkney and Northern Europe in the Later Iron Age* AD *300–800*, 11–19. Balgavies.

Carter, S. 1993. Tulloch Wood, Forres, Moray: The survey and dating of a fragment of prehistoric landscape, *Proc Soc Antiq Scot*, 123 (1993), 215–33.

Cavers, G., Heald, A. & Barber, J. *forthcoming* 'Monuments and Memory in the Iron Age of Caithness', in Stoddart, S & Malone, C (eds) *Gardening Time: the Iron Age in Scotland and Sardinia*. Oxford.

Childe, V. G. 1943. Another late Viking house at Freswick, Caithness, *Proc Soc Antiq. Scot*, 77 (1942–43), 5–17.

Clark, H. & Sellers, R. M. 2005. *The Birds and Mammals of Caithness: Robert Innes Shearer's Contribution to the Natural History of Caithness, 1859–1867*. Wick.

Clarke, D. V. 2002. 'The foremost figure in all matters relating to Scottish archaeology': Aspects of the work of Joseph Anderson (1832–1916), *Proc Soc Antiq Scot*, 132 (2002), 1–18.

Close-Brooks, J. 1975. Two bronzes from Caithness, *Proc Soc Antiq Scot*, 106 (1974–5), 194–5.

Close-Brooks, J. 1984. Pictish and other burials, in Friell, J. G. P. & Watson, W. G. (eds), *Pictish Studies. Settlement, Burial and Art in Dark Age Northern Britain*, 87–114 (= BAR British Ser 125, Oxford).

Coles, J. 1960. Scottish Late Bronze Age metalwork: Typology, distribution and chronology, *Proc Soc Antiq Scot*, 93 (1959–60), 16–134.

Coles, J. 1964. Scottish Middle Bronze Age bronzework, *Proc Soc Antiq Scot*, 97 (1963–64), 82–156.

Coles, J. M. 1969. Scottish Early Bronze Age metalwork, *Proc Soc Antiq Scot*, 101 (1968–69), 1–110.

Corcoran, J.X.W.P. 1966. Excavation of three chambered cairns at Loch Calder, Caithness, *Pro Soc Antiq Scot*, 98 (1964–66), 1–75

Cowan, E. J. 1982. Caithness in the Sagas, in Baldwin, J. R. (ed), *Caithness. A Cultural Crossroads*, 25–44. Edinburgh.

Cowley, D. C. 1998. Identifying marginality in the first and second millennia BC in the Strath of Kildonan, Sutherland, in Mills, C. M. & Coles, G. (eds), *Life on the Edge: Human Settlement and Marginality*, 165–71. Oxford (=Oxbow Mongr 100).

Cowley, D.C. 1999. Squaring the circle: Domestic architecture in Later Prehistoric Sutherland and Caithness, in Frodsham, P., Topping, P. & Cowley, D. (eds), *We Were Always Chasing Time. Papers Presented to Keith Blood, Northern Archaeology*, 17/18, 67–75.

Cowley, D. 2005. Architecture, landscape and the political geography of Iron Age Caithness and Sutherland, in Turner, V., Nicholson, R. A., Dockrill, S. J. & Bond, J. M. (eds), *Tall Stories? Two Millennia of Brochs*, 180–9. Shetland.

Cree, J. E. 1911. Notice of the excavation of a hut circle near Ackergill Tower, Wick, Caithness, *Proc Soc Antiq Scot*, 45 (1910–11), 181–6.

Crone, A. 2012. Forging a chronological framework for Scottish crannogs; the radiocarbon and dendrochronological evidence, in Midgley, M. & Sanders, J. (eds) *Lake-dwellings after Robert Munro*, 139–68. Sidestone Press, Leiden, The Netherlands.

Curle, A. O. 1912. Excavation of a galleried structure at Langwell, Caithness', *Proc Soc Antiq Scot*, 46 (1911–12), 77–89.

Curle, A. O. 1913 'Two penannular gold armlets, and the stone bowl in which they were found, from Hillhead, Caithness', *Proc Soc Antiq Scot*, 47 (1912–13), 433–5.

Curle, A. O. 1914. Report on the excavation of a vitrified fort at Rockcliffe, Dalbeattie, known as the Mote of Mark, *Proc Soc Antiq Scot*, 48 (1913–4), 125–68.

Curle, A. O. 1932. Interim report on the excavation of a Bronze Age dwelling at Yarlshof, Shetland in 1931, *Proc Soc Antiq Scot*, 66 (1931–2), 113–28.

Curle, A. O. 1933. Account of further excavation in 1932 of the prehistoric township at Jarlshof, Shetland, on Behalf of H. M. Office of Works, *Proc Soc Antiq Scot*, 67 (1932–3), 82–136.

Curle, A. O. 1934. An account of further excavations at Jarlshof, Shetland in 1932 and 1933, on behalf of H. M. Office of Works, *Proc Soc Antiq Scot*, 68 (1933–4), 224–319.

Curle, A. O. 1939. A Viking settlement at Freswick, Caithness. Report on the excavations carried on in 1937 and 1938, *Proc Soc Antiq Scot*, 73 (1938–9), 71–110.

Curle, A. O. 1941. An account of the partial excavation of a 'wag' or galleried building at Forse, in the parish of Latheron, Caithness, *Proc Soc Antiq Scot*, 75 (1940–1), 23–39.

Curle, A. O. 1946. The excavation of the 'wag' or prehistoric cattle-fold at Forse, Caithness and the relation of 'wags' to brochs, and implications arising therefrom, *Proc Soc Antiq Scot*, 80 (1945–6), 11–25.

Curle, A. O. 1948. The 'wag' of Forse, Caithness: Excavations 1947–48, *Proc Soc Antiq Scot*, 82 (1947–8), 275–86.

Curle, A. O. & Cree, J. E. 1916. Account of excavations on Traprain Law in the parish of Prestonkirk, county of Haddington, in 1915, *Proc Soc Antiq Scot*, 50 (1915–16), 64–144.

Curle, J. 1914. On recent Scandinavian grave-finds from the Island of Oronsay, and from Reay, Caithness, with notes on the development and chronology of the oval brooch of the Viking time, *Proc Soc Antiq Scot*, 48 (1913–14), 292–315.

Davidson, J. L. & Henshall, A. S. 1991. *The Chambered Cairns of Caithness*. Edinburgh.

Dockrill, S. 2007. *Investigations in Sanday, Orkney Vol 2: Tofts Ness, Sanday, an Island Landscape through 3000 Years of Prehistory.* The Orcadian Ltd and Historic Scotland.

Dutton, A. 2003. Hill o' Many Stanes (Mid Clyth), *Discovery and Excavation Scotland (DES)*, 4, 89–90.

Edwards, A. J. H. 1926. Excavation of a number of graves in a mound at Ackergill, Caithness, *Proc Soc Antiq Scot*, 60 (1925–6), 160–82.

Edwards, A. J. H. 1927. Excavations of graves at Ackergill and of an earth-house at Freswick Links, Caithness, and a description of the discovery of a Viking grave at Reay, Caithness, *Proc Soc Antiq Scot*, 61 (1926–27), 196–209.

Edwards, A. J. H. 1929. Excavations at Reay Links and at a horned cairn at Lower Dounreay, Caithness, *Proc Soc Antiq Scot*, 63 (1928–29), 138–49.

Fairhurst, H. 1984. *Excavations at Crosskirk, Caithness*. Edinburgh (=Soc Antiq Scot Monogr Ser, 3).

Fairhurst, H. & Taylor, D. B. 1971. A hut circle settlement at Kilpheder, Sutherland, *Proc Soc Antiq Scot*, 103 (1970–1), 65–99.

Fojut, N. 1981. Is Mousa a Broch? *Proc Soc Antiq Scot*, 111 (1981), 220–8.

Foster, S. M. 1989. Transformations in social space: Iron Age Orkney and Caithness, *Scot Archaeol Rev*, 6 (1989), 34–55.

Freer, R. & Myatt, L. J. 1982. The multiple stone rows of Caithness and Sutherland, *Caithness Field Club Bulletin*, 3 (1982), 58–67.

Gourlay, R. 1984. A symbol stone and cairn at Watenan, Caithness, in Friell, J. G. P. & Watson, W. G (eds), *Pictish Studies. Settlement, Burial and Art in Dark Age Northern Britain*, 131–4 (= BAR British Ser 125, Oxford).

Graham, A. 1976. The archaeology of Joseph Anderson, *Proc Soc Antiq Scot*, 107 (1975–76), 279–98.

Graham-Campbell, J. & Batey, C. 1998. *Vikings in Scotland: an Archaeological Survey*. Edinburgh.

Greig, C., Greig, M. & Ashmore, P. 2000. Excavation of a cairn cemetery at Lundin Links, Fife in 1965–6, *Proc Soc Antiq Scot*, 130 (2000), 585–636.

Grieg, S. 1940. Viking antiquities in Scotland, in Shetelig, H (ed.) *Viking Antiquities in Great Britain and Ireland* (Part 2), H. Aschehoug & Co., Oslo.

Gunn, G. 1915. *The Standing Stones of Caithness*. Transactions of the Inverness Field Club. Inverness.

Harding, D. W. 2004. *The Iron Age in Northern Britain: Celts and Romans, Natives and Invaders.* London and New York.

Heald, A. & Jackson, A. 2001. Towards a new understanding of Iron Age Caithness, *Proc Soc Antiq Scot*, 131 (2001), 129–47.

Heald, A. & Jackson, A. 2002. Caithness Archaeological Project: Excavations at Everley Broch, Freswick, *Antiquity*, 76 (2002), 31–2.

Hedges, J. W. 1987. *Bu, Gurness and the Broch of Orkney Vol 1–3*. Oxford (= BAR Brit Ser 163–5).

Henshall, A. 1963. *The Chambered Tombs of Scotland*, Volume 1. Edinburgh University Press, Edinburgh.

Henshall, A. 1972. *The Chambered Tombs of Scotland*, Volume 2. Edinburgh University Press, Edinburgh.

Hopkinson, S. 1994. *Roast Chicken and Other Stories*. London.

Joass, J. M. 1890. The brochs or 'pictish towers' of Cinn-Trolla, Carn-Liath, and Craig-Carril, in Sutherland, with notes on other northern brochs, *Archaeol Scot*, 5 (1890), 95–130.

Laing, L, Oakley, E, Sassin, A E & Tompsett, I 2013 'Excavations at the Early and later Medieval site of Ballachly, Dunbeath, Caithness, 2007–2010', *Proc Soc Antiq Scot*, 143 (2013), 265–302.

Laing, S. 1868. On the age of the burgs or "brochs" and some other Prehistoric remains of Orkney and Caithness, *Proc Soc Antiq Scot*, 7 (1866–8), 56–79.

Laing, S. 1885. *Modern Science and Modern Thought*. London.

Laing, S. 1889. *Problems of the Future*. London.

Laing, S. 1892. *Human Origins*. London.

Laing, S. & Huxley, T. H. 1866. *Prehistoric Remains of Caithness*. Edinburgh.

Lamb, R. G. 1980. *Iron Age Promontory Forts in the Northern Isles*. Oxford (=Brit Archaeol Rep, 79).

Love, P. 1989. Recent excavations at Carn Liath Broch, Golspie, Sutherland, *Glasgow Archaeol J*, 15 (1988–89), 157–69.

Lowe, C. 1998. *St Boniface Church Orkney. Coastal Erosion and Archaeological Assessment*. Stroud.

Macallister. R. A. S.1928. *The Archaeology of Ireland*, Methuen, London.

McCullagh, R. P. J. & Tipping, R. 1998. *The Lairg project 1988–1996: the evolution of an archaeological landscape in northern Scotland. Edinburgh*, Scottish Trust for Archaeological Research.

MacKay, J. 1892. Notice of the Excavation of the Broch at Ousdale, Caithness, *Proc Soc Antiq Scot*, 26 (1891–2), 351–7.

MacKie, E. W. 1974. *Dun Mor Vaul: an Iron Age Broch on Tiree*. Glasgow.

MacKie, E. W. 1994. Gurness and Midhowe Brochs in Orkney: Some problems of misinterpretation, *Archaeol J*, 151 (1994), 98–157.

MacKie, E. W. 2000. The Scottish Atlantic Iron Age; indigenous and isolated or part of a wider European World? in Henderson, J. (ed), *The Prehistory and Early History of Atlantic Europe: Papers from a Session Held at the European Association of Archaeologists Fourth Annual Meeting in Goteborg 1998*, 99–116. Oxford: BAR International Series 861.

MacKie, E. W. 2002. *The Roundhouses, Brochs and Wheelhouses of Atlantic Scotland c.700 BC – AD 500: Architecture and Material Culture Part 1 – The Orkney and Shetland Isles*. Oxford (=Brit Archaeol Rep, 342).

MacKie, E. W. 2007. *The Roundhouses, Brochs and Wheelhouses of Atlantic Scotland c.700 BC to AD 500. Architecture and material culture. Part 2 (I) The Northern & Southern Mainland and the Western Islands*. Oxford (=BAR British Series, 444).

McLuhan, M. & Fiore, Q. 1967. *The Medium is the Massage*. Harmondsworth.

Masters, L. 1997. The excavation and restoration of the Camster Long chambered cairn, Caithness, Highland, 1967–80, *Proc Soc Antiq Scot*, 127 (1997), 123–83.

Mercer, R. 1980. *Archaeological Field Survey in Northern Scotland 1976–1979*. Edinburgh (=Univ Edinburgh Archaeol Dept Occas Pap, 4).

Mercer, R. 1981. *Archaeological Field Survey in Northern Scotland. Volume II, 1980–1*. Edinburgh (=Univ Edinburgh Archaeol Dept Occas Pap, 7).

Mercer, R. 1985 *Archaeological Field Survey in Northern Scotland. Volume III, 1982–3*. Edinburgh (=Univ Edinburgh Archaeol Dept Occas Pap, 11).

Mens, E. 2008. Refitting megaliths in western France, *Antiquity*, 82 (2008), 25.

Morris, C., Batey, C. & Rackham, D. J. 1995. *Freswick Links, Caithness. Excavation and Survey of a Norse Settlement*. Stroud.

Morrison, A. 1996. *Dunbeath: A Cultural Landscape*. Dunbeath Preservation Trust/Department of Archaeology (= University of Glasgow Occas Pap, 3).

Mulville, J., Parker Pearson, M., Sharples, N., Smith, H. & Chamberlain, A. 2003. Quarters, arcs and squares: Human and animal remains in the Hebridean Late Iron Age', in Downes, J. & Ritchie, A. (eds), *Sea Change: Orkney and Northern Europe in the Later Iron Age AD 300–800*, 20–34. Balgavies.

Munro, R. 1882. *Ancient Scottish Lake-dwellings or Crannogs: With a Supplementary Chapter on Remains of Lake-dwellings in England*. Edinburgh.

Mowat, J. 1912. *Caithness Sketches*. Glasgow Caithness Literary Association Mowat.

Myatt, L. 1988. The stone rows of northern Scotland, in Ruggles, C. L. N.(ed), *Records in Stone. Papers in Memory of Alexander Thom*, 277–318. Cambridge.

Myatt, L. 1992. Stone rows and stone circles, in Omand, D. (ed), *The New Caithness Book*, 40–6. Wick.

Myatt, L. 2003. *The Stone Rows of Caithness. A Guide*. Wick.

Nicolson, J. 1916. The Exploration of the Site known as the Kirk Stones of Stroupster, in the parish of Wick, county of Caithness, *Proc Soc Antiq Scot*, 50 (1915–16), 314–16.

Nicolson, J. 1922. A cross-slab found at St John's Chapel, Canisbay, Caithness, *Proc Soc Antiq Scot*, 56 (1921–22), 66–7.

Omand, D. 1989. *The New Caithness Book*. Wick: North of Scotland Newspapers. First edition.

Pannett, A. & Baines, A. 2006. 'Making Things, Making Places: The Excavation of Mesolithic Flint Knapping Sites at Oliclett, Caithness', Scot Archaeol JL, 1 (2006), 1–26.

Parker Pearson, M & Sharples, N 1999. *Between Land and Sea: Excavations at Dun Vulan, South Uist*, Sheffield.

Phillips, T. 2002. *Landscapes of the Living, Landscapes of the Dead: The Location of Chambered Cairns of Northern Scotland*. Oxford (=British Archaeological Reports (BAR), British Series 328).

Pollard, T. 1999. The sands of time: The investigation of a Norse settlement at Dunnet Bay, Caithness, in Frodsham, P., Topping, P. & Cowley, D. (eds), *We Were Always Chasing Time. Papers Presented to Keith Blood, Northern Archaeology*, 17/18, 149–57.

Price, T. D., Grupe, G. & Schröter, P. 1998. 'Migration in the Bell Beaker period of central Europe', *Antiquity*, 72, issue 276 (1998), 405–411.

RCAHMS 1911. *Royal Commission of the Ancient and Historical Monuments of Scotland. Caithness. Vol III*, Edinburgh.

RCAHMS 1998. *The Sir Francis Tress Barry Collection. Catalogue of Material Held in the National Monuments Record of Scotland*. Edinburgh.

Renfrew, A. C. 1979. *Investigations in Orkney*. London (= Society of Antiquaries of London, Research Report No. 38).

Rhind, A. H. 1853. Notice of the exploration of a 'Picts house' at Kettleburn, in the county of Caithness', *Arch Jl*, 10 (1853), 212–23.

Rhind, A. H. 1854a. An account of an extensive collection of archaeological relics, and osteological remains, from a 'Pict's house' at Kettleburn, Caithness, *Proc Soc Antiq Scot*, 1 (1851–4), 264–69.

Rhind, A. H. 1854b. Results of excavations in sepulchral cairns in the north of Scotland, identical in internal design with the great chambered tumuli on the banks of the Boyne, in Ireland, *Ulster J Archaeol*, 2, 100–108.

Ritchie, A. 2011. Cemeteries of platform cairns and long cists around Sinclair's Bay, Caithness, *Proc Soc Antiq Scot*, 141 (2011), 125–43.

Ritchie, J. N. G. 2002. James Curle (1862–1944) and Alexander Ormiston Curle (1866–1955): pillars of the establishment, *Proc Soc Antiq Scot*, 132 (2002), 19–41.

Scott, B. G. 1977. Dancing, Drink or Drugs? Comments on the 'Beaker Cult-Package' Hypothesis, *Irish Archaeological Research Forum*, 4, (1977), 29–34.

Sharples, N. 1984. Excavations at Pierowall Quarry, Westray, Orkney, *Proc Soc Antiq Scot*, (1984), 75–125.

Sharples, N. 1998. *Scalloway: A Broch, Late Iron Age Settlement and Medieval Cemetery in Shetland*, Oxford (Oxbow Monogr, 82).

Sheridan, A. 2008. Radiocarbon dates arranged through National Museums Scotland Archaeology Department during 2007/8, *Discovery and Excavation in Scotland*, 9 (2008), 201–205.

Stuart, J. 1864. *Memoir of Alexander Henry Rhind of Sibster*. Edinburgh.

Stuart, J. 1868. Report to the committee of the Society of Antiquaries of Scotland, appointed to arrange for the application of a fund left by the late Mr. A. Henry Rhind, for excavating early remains, *Proc Soc Antiq Scot*, 7 (1866–8), 289–307.

Swanson, C. 1992. The brochs, in Omand, D. (ed), *The New Caithness Book*, 47–55. Wick.

Thom, A. 1971. *Megalithic Lunar Observatories*. Oxford

Thom, A., Thom, A. S. & Burl, A. 1990. Stone rows and standing stones. Britain, Ireland and Brittany. Part II. Oxford (=BAR Inter Ser 560(ii))

Tucker, F. & Armit, I. 2009. 'Human Remains from Iron Age Atlantic Scotland Dating Project: Results obtained during 2009', *Discovery and Excavation in Scotland*, 10 (2009), 214–216.

Waugh, D. 1992. 'Place-names', in Omand (ed), *The New Caithness Book*, 141–155.

Williams, H. 2007. Depicting the dead: commemoration through cists, cairns and symbols in early medieval Britain, *Cambridge Archaeol Jl*, 17(2), 145–64.

Wilson, D. 1863. *Prehistoric Annals of Scotland. Volume II*. Edinburgh.

LIST OF ILLUSTRATIONS

INDEX

NB: page numbers in italics indicate illustrations

A NEW WAY OF LIVING
Georgian Town Planning in the Highlands and Islands

- A study of the origins of the revolution in social and physical planning in the Highlands and Islands

- Reveals the rationale for the expansive building programme post-1750 and identifies key personnel

- Analyses the qualities of urban form of selected towns in relation to the original plans

- Considers the detail of current plans for new town and questions their logic

available from
www.whittlespublishing.com

READING THE GAELIC LANDSCAPE
Leughadh Aghaidh na Tìre

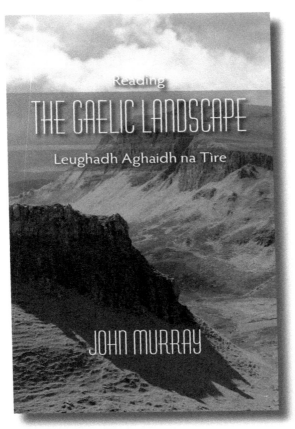

- ...essential for those interested in the Highlands and its ancient, living language. It helps readers and outdoor enthusiasts understand seemingly obscure words on maps, with insights into landscape history and ecology. *The Scots Magazine*

- ...Murray's book reminds us how deep the natural environment is within the Gaelic soul; how virtually every hillock, stream and bay in the Gael's place will have been named at some point. These names are windows allowing glimpses of our forebears. *David Ross, The Herald*

- ...John Murray's book is unique is synthesising everything that has gone before and adding a great deal that is new in an attempt to allow those unfamiliar with the language a genuine insight into the name of every type of landscape and mapping feature. The result is a triumph. ... Just occasionally you come across a book whose lasting value is so obvious that you know people will be referring to it in 50 years' time or more. Reading the Gaelic Landscape is one of those books. *Undiscovered Scotland*

 available from
www.whittlespublishing.com